3|19

SARAH McCOLL

JOY
enough

A Memoir

LIVERIGHT PUBLISHING CORPORATION
A Division of W. W. Norton & Company
Independent Publishers Since 1923
NEW YORK · LONDON

Excerpt from "Amy Hempel, The Art of Fiction No. 176" interview by
Paul Winner, originally published in *The Paris Review,* Issue 166, Summer 2003.
Copyright © 2003 The Paris Review, used by permission
of The Wylie Agency LLC.

For information about permission to reproduce selections from this book, write to
Permissions, Liveright Publishing Corporation, a division of
W. W. Norton & Company, Inc., 500 Fifth Avenue, New York, NY 10110

For information about special discounts for bulk purchases, please contact
W. W. Norton Special Sales at specialsales@wwnorton.com or 800-233-4830

Manufacturing by LSC Communications, Harrisonburg
Book design by Ellen Cipriano
Production manager: Anna Oler

ISBN 978-1-63149-470-3

Liveright Publishing Corporation, 500 Fifth Avenue, New York, N.Y. 10110
www.wwnorton.com

W. W. Norton & Company Ltd., 15 Carlisle Street, London W1D 3BS

1 2 3 4 5 6 7 8 9 0

For Duncan, Katy, and Bliss

Some writers have a more defined sense of cause and effect. Plot. My sense of life is more moment, moment, and moment. Looking back, they accrue and occur to you at a certain time and maybe you don't know why, but you trust that they are coming back to you now for a reason. And you make a leap of faith. You trust you can put these moments together and create story.

—Amy Hempel

Finally, the lessons of impermanence taught me this: loss constitutes an odd kind of fullness; despair empties out into an unquenchable appetite for life.

—Gretel Ehrlich

The mere sense of living is joy enough.

—Emily Dickinson

winter

LOVED MY MOTHER, and she died. Is that a story?

Story is giving a character a tangible desire, then putting things in her way. A writer I was falling in love with told me that. My desire is for my mother to live. *More tangible*, he says. My desire is not to forget. *More tangible*, he says.

Then my desire is for her to meet the next man I love, the one I keep now that I know a thing or two. My desire is for her to see my round silhouette in a summer dress, then to hold my baby in the delivery room. In winter, my desire is to make chili with the mixture of garden tomatoes and hot peppers she calls *hell* that I've kept in the back of my freezer. Our desires are equally impossible: to freeze hell, to thaw it; to reverse time, to stop it. My desire is to have more of what I do not need, seconds of what has been my fair share: a fight, a car ride, a cup of coffee, ignored advice straight from the mouth of a grade A know-it-all.

Or none of this. My desire is preservation, to carry her lodged beneath my breast like a bone.

More tangible, he says.

H ER NAME WAS Allison, but her father called her Tune. My little petunia, he said.

It was like living in a green bowl, she said, the way the valley
curved out a hollow at the foot of Mt. Greylock, and another ridge
rose behind the barn and silo, enclosing their loneliness. The
sphere at the end of the banister was the size of a boy's face and
about the right height. She leaned in with eyes closed to practice.
Ridgeview Farm was in Western Massachusetts, five long, hilly
miles outside of Williamstown along the cold Green River. She let
the screen door bang on her way out to the pasture.

The air was manure and hay. It smelled of warm earth, of
growing things. How do you round up cows? They are docile
but slow moving, recalcitrant, with calves at their sides like small
shadows. Maybe she called them by name or had the help of a
dog, but somehow she herded those somnolent beasts into the
barn where there were quiet stalls lined with stiff straw, and birds
sat overhead in the eaves of the aluminum roof. Somehow she
convinced them that was where they wanted to be.

It was not where she wanted to be. She felt the ache at every
age, when she played house with a family of her own imagined
children and performed from a rock to an audience of dumb daylilies. Her father shook the ice in his bourbon-and-gingers while
he told jokes at a dinner table tight with seven plates of spaghetti.
But the neighborhood was empty of anyone who wasn't a relative
or slow-talking farmer. Just as her mother escaped to town each
morning to swivel around an office, Tune rode a bike into thick
woods. Under a slow-waving canopy, the light came through in
patches. Mother and daughter's longing was shared but unspoken.

When Tune was an adult and her own mother died, the parked cars overflowed onto the road's grassy shoulder, and four college presidents stood in the back of the church. Tune didn't cry. She had lost her mother a long time ago, she said, when she understood her mother was not the kind she had needed. This is one kind of mother and daughter.

She and I are another.

WHEN PEOPLE SAY, tell me about your mother, which they never do, I say she was my spiritual home.

So to say I miss her—which I often did in the months following her death, because I did not have the language to express my roiling grief—was a polite way of calling myself a cosmic orphan, like a moon whose planet has fallen out of orbit.

My physical home: Sixth Avenue in Brooklyn, where I mark time by the trees, one in particular. The willow at Fifteenth Street is lush with long, falling maiden hair, its boughs rustling in the thawed breeze like underskirts across a polished wood dance floor. My husband moved out three months before my mother died, when the snow was still on the ground. Since then, I live alone.

But in the first weeks of spring, a heavy perfume hangs in the air on the corner of Fourteenth Street, and I stop on the sidewalk outside the Italian restaurant. Honeysuckle. The thick fragrance is unmistakable, but I cannot see the blooms, as if someone is calling my name who has not yet stepped into view.

W E REHEARSE OUR adult lives from the beginning. Mine was a game in the front yard. Into a bucket go sharp holly leaves, cedar chips from the flower beds, errant sticks, fistfuls of clover—never can find the lucky ones—rippled pink blooms from the crape myrtles, and pale yellow honeysuckle blossoms. The bush forms a lush border between our house and the neighbors next door. One for me to eat; the stamen like a slide whistle and tongue touched to the drop of nectar. One for the bucket, and the blossom drifts to join the lawn detritus. The afternoon is a quiet expanse, the house emptied of my older brother and sister at school, my younger brother not yet born. I pause to watch doodlebugs dawdle along the pebbled surface of our front porch. Then into the kitchen, where my mother smears peanut butter on white bread, drips honey, and sinks a knife to cut fours. It is just the two of us, and I am out to make something, too. My bucket slides under the tap, there is a rush of hot water, and I stand as if at a cauldron with my witch's brew, stirring with a wooden spoon until there is a fierce swirl at the center. *Lunch*, she says, and my sandwich is on a blue and white plate. *Stew!* I announce, vainglorious at my own creation.

H ER FIRST MEMORY is of ants, of watching a single-file parade inside the trumpet of a daylily. Theirs is a bicentennial farm. For two hundred years a single family has pushed orchard apples through a food mill and lined the cellar shelves with canned pole beans, slipped from the barn roof, and died in labor. When my mother is older, she will bring her own diapered children to the top of the same hill and slide daylilies behind our ears, and many years after that, I will sneak away with my husband from a barbecue and lie down with him in the shadow of a tractor. But the first thing she remembers, she tells me, is the ants, their fluid line like pen ink, a whole city inside a bloom. It is June, and the sheets are snapping dry on the clothesline.

This is a memory of a memory, an image of my mother's childhood inside an image of my own, like nesting *matryoshkas*. When I hear about the ants, my mother is dropping me off at school. I am in fifth grade and fat, and Anne Murray's *Greatest Hits* is in the tape deck of her white Ford Taurus. I have a lavender backpack with neon zippers on my lap, and even I know it looks cheap. It's raining, and I am nearly late for the second bell, the drop-off traffic snaking around the block, and my mother won't stop talking.

Your first memory, she goes on, is significant. She's getting her masters in social work and spends the evenings hammering away at her typewriter, smoking cigarettes. I don't ask what she thinks her ants mean. This is how she and I talk, about what things mean, but today I'm distracted—by the time, by the distance to the side door if I get out of the car and run, and mostly by the rain, which will soak my white t-shirt, under which I am not wearing a bra because no one but me has yet noticed I need one.

The adults in my life are themselves distracted. My father drives a Cadillac as long and silver as a shark. But last week he picked me up for Wednesday night Hamburger Helper at his apartment wearing pants I'd never seen with a hole in the crotch.

He talked about money, why Christmas would be different this year, and asked why my mother keeps writing hot checks at the grocery store. I don't know what a hot check is.

The morning in the car my mother asks what my first memory is and waits for the answer like it matters, the windshield wipers like a metronome. How is a memory different from a photograph or a story you've been told about yourself? I am nine going on ten and beginning to get angry, not just at the rain that morning or the delay, but at a growing sense of life's unfairness. Our house is filled with moving boxes, and letters from my father's law office arrive by courier at the front door. I am more interested in visions of on and on, like this: I imagine sitting in front of a television. On the screen is a person watching television of another person, seated on a couch, watching television. And so on. I tell my mother I would like to minor in philosophy. She thinks this is funny, but I find it all very deep.

W E ONLY EVER WRITE one story, the writer I was beginning to love told me. Several months after my mother's death, looking through stacks of paper in her sewing room, I found a yellow folder. "The Life of Allison Marie Young," she wrote in felt-tipped calligraphy pen, "by her daughter, Sarah." This was my third-grade project. *Tell me what you were like when you were my age*, I asked, then neatly wrote the most interesting parts on ruled notebook paper beside crayon illustrations. She sank a homemade raft in the Green River and sat astride her cousin Bonnie's pony.

Bonnie looked good in cheap clothes, my mother always said, and that's all I know about Bonnie.

Tell me what you were like when you were my age, I asked in high school. We did most of our talking in the warmth of the car, waiting for a school bus that stopped a distance from our house. My mother wore her nightgown beneath a down parka and spilled tea on the floorboards. On the first hot day, the scent of sour milk haunted the car. She babysat, she said, and when the kids went to sleep, she ate leftovers from the fridge, didn't wash the dishes though she had a feeling she was supposed to, and thumbed the parents' copy of *Tropic of Cancer* for the sex parts.

Ice crystals scattered on the windows like field-borne burrs. I had woken that morning from a dream, I told her, in which I stood in a tunnel, my arms wrapped inside the peacoat of a boy as a train barreled toward us. "Well, that's obviously about sex," she said. And then, "Here comes the bus." I slumped on and into the first seat, perturbed. She could decode my subconscious, so why did hers seem so opaque? I wrote a poem, which is what sixteen-year-olds do, and left it at her place at the kitchen table one night before bed.

"Dear Sarah," she wrote in a letter she slid under my bedroom door. "If it seems that I am vague about my childhood, forgive me. It's only that there is not much to tell. I was dreamy and lonely and liked to read magazines and ride my bike."

I did not know how to ask a question impossible to answer. Can you explain what people mean when they say, *You are just like your mother?*

Now she is dead, and unable to answer, and still I cannot stop. There is comfort in asking. The possibility of discovery seems, at once, as real as the night sky and as difficult to measure as love.

Another surprise sewing room find, the motherlode: beside the plush camel chair she dozed in at the end, her head tipped back into the afternoon sun, a bag from Stop and Shop. It was overstuffed and heavy, filled with knitting needles, leather-bound journals, drafts of letters to doctors, friends, her therapist, my father. There were five copies of her divorce papers, and two day planners from the 1980s. Neon Post-its popped from the pages like flags.

"Hope now?" she wrote on a small piece of lined, mono-grammed notepaper in her thirties. "That I won't just die and become fertilizer—that I won't be forgotten as if I had never lived. That I'll give good people to the world. That things will become clearer to me, that I'll understand better. It really bugs me that I don't understand everything already."

It bugs me, too.

S HE TOLD THE STORY the same way each time, with the fresh-ness of someone relaying details the next morning from a dormitory hall phone. Now seems as good a time as any to men-tion she was an unreliable narrator, but here we go.

Heat blasted through the vents in the dashboard and the win-dows fogged with their girl talk, headlights blunted by a vortex of snowflakes. Someone reapplied lipstick while someone else announced street names as the signs came into view. My mother buttoned her purple maxi coat. The heavy dorm door creaked open, and my father stood in the stony hallway with a thick red beard.

I could feel his hot breath on my cold cheeks as he said, "Would you like a cup of coffee?"

When my father was on chapel duty, they sat in the back pew, cookies inside their coat pockets. He was so handsome, one of my mother's classmates said later, she wanted to put his head on her mantle.

This was one of my mother's truisms: A person will reveal everything you need to know about them within the first twenty minutes. The trick is whether or not you're paying attention.

After coffee, my mother grabbed a toothbrush and toothpaste from her purse.

Don't you want the flavor to linger in your mouth? my father asked.

On she went to the bathroom, maybe noticing a moment where pleasure locked horns with practicality, but maybe not.

And so it was the same for me, a daughter like a rerun.

"It's weird, Allison," one of her classmates said at a reunion, when I was my mother's date, flipping through magazines on a dorm room floor and swinging my legs in the air. "It's like it's you thirty years ago there on the floor."

FOR TEN YEARS, I was crazy about one man. He becomes my husband. I go wild for his hands, the way he ties a square knot, and how, when he holds a drink, he smiles at me slyly from the side of his mouth.

Just like my parents, dumb with infatuation and blind to early evidence of their failed future, my husband and I can't see what's clearly coming: that he will spend more time writing code at his computer than in my company, that I am relatively unambitious, and, not Chinese.

When we're in the dark of it I say, "Let's do something fun." And because we are so far down, I don't even know what that might mean. So I ask him, "What's fun?"

"Fun is noodles," he answers, his Chinese mother's phrase. Chow fun, mei fun. The only way to have it is to eat it. A month later he has emptied his closet, and two months after that he pushes a thick manila envelope under the door of our apartment. Inside, divorce papers and a bar of dark chocolate. Not fun.

Each morning, I slip a silk blouse over my head and ride the subway to an office in midtown. I am the editor in chief of a website about food, and I cannot eat. In the office bathroom, I sink to my feet. At my desk, I lean my head toward my knees. My mother says my body is processing the pain.

And then one day, because I cannot bear masking my personal mess at the office again, I get off the D train at Grand Street by the stinky fish vendors and walk across Nolita to a coffee shop on Mott Street. When I swing the door open, I look up into the face of a man.

"Hi," I say. I am breathless from the cold.

"Hi," he answers, and he bares his teeth like a friendly wolf.

I think I can feel his hot breath on my cheeks.

We do not fall in love. Or we do, and it doesn't last. What matters is this: I've been slapped by white sun, and for weeks my mind is blank-frantic, whirling like an empty spin cycle. Yet what I feel is full.

Call this boy-crazy, as I usually do, and it's a bone-deep embarrassment. Call it the life force, as my mother did, and it's elemental—proof I am alive, that the heart beating inside this chest is a woman's.

HERE'S SOMETHING a woman can do: birth boy, girl, girl, boy. I am that second girl. She let the first three of us unfurl with random assignment of Xs and Ys. For the fourth, she got serious. She wanted us lined up like von Trapps, longed for two more sons but would settle for one. Her old-timer gynecologist had strategies to determine sex, and so my mother nodded, sitting in a cotton gown on his examining table, the opening in front. He mailed instructions, the letter stamped at the post office on June 27, 1986. Postage was twenty-two cents.

"To favor conception of a male: (1) Intercourse at or as close to ovulation as possible with prior abstinence during the cycle, immediately preceded by an alkaline douche of water and baking soda. (2) Intercourse with female orgasm. (3) Deep penetration at the time of emission."

Now for the fun part. It must have been the following January when my mother placed a call to my father's law office saying he was needed at home. He was due in court, so when he hung up, he placed a call of his own. *Your Honor*, he said, and told the truth. More remarkable still, it worked. That is the story of how we got my little brother, Bliss, and how we became a complete set.

We made our home in glitzy Dallas, where only maids waited at bus stops, though we did not call them maids, we called them housekeepers. In our neighborhood, sixteen-year-olds woke to luxury cars in the driveway, the hoods festooned with giant red bows. My mother enlivened errands with a new bumper sticker: NUCLEAR WASTE IS FOREVER. At night, my parents fantasized about returning to San Antonio or Austin, where they had been young and poor and happy. We stay.

Ours was a monkey house. Someone was naked or dropping the fire ladder from a third floor window to escape. There was dog shit on the Oriental rug and an empty roll of paper towels. My mother weaved herself in with husband and kids in a water-tight web. We hollered down the hallway, shoved. She said, *Give your sister a hug and say you're sorry*, and we rolled our eyes. When the country station was on in the kitchen after dinner, my parents danced the push. My father's loafers shuffled across the black and white tile floor. The soles sounded like leaves rustling along a riverside. Farm lore says when the silver undersides turn face up, it's going to rain.

Problems: a husband who flexed in the mirror each morning after swimming laps, a tony town of Joneses she didn't care to keep up with, and even with all those kids, that same dogged loneliness followed. There was a longing still. If the farm of her youth was cloaked in a kind of quiet separateness, at least the family she made felt different, loud, and braided like a lasso.

My older brother says our parents' bedroom door was locked for most of his childhood. "I thought it was because they were Democrats," he said.

"Your mother must *love* being pregnant," my Brownies troop

leader said when my mother pulled up in our red Suburban, the other three already in the car.

My sister came home for college vacation and announced on the way to buy spring dresses that the vagina was a hole. She'd read something. I was fifteen and in the backseat.

"The vagina is not a hole," my mother said. "The vagina is a vessel."

She sewed wrap skirts she could wear at any size waist, chose colors for the baby's room, supervised sleepovers. There's a photograph of her pregnant at a picnic. She has one hand on her belly, another holding a glass of iced tea, the red curls at her temples damp with sweat. My sister is inside, my brother at her feet, still in diapers.

Introduced at a cocktail party or turning to a fellow dinner guest, she could see the boredom in their eyes when she said she was a mother. But hers was the real work, she thought, the kind that defines a civilization. Her materials were empty toilet paper rolls smeared in peanut butter, rolled in birdseed, and hung from the honeysuckle bush outside the dining room window.

"The thought of life after my children are grown depresses me. I will probably read some and drink a whole lot," she wrote. She thought there might be a novel in this about a thirty-nine-year-old woman who doesn't want to stop having children. "But I don't know where the plot would take her."

Husband and wife are both blue, really. They see a marriage counselor. The early diagnosis is that she is grieving the end of childbearing. "But I wonder if I really want more children, or if I just want to be sure I remember all the joyfulness I've felt."

To remember all the joy.

TWICE A WEEK she takes her two-year-old to swimming lessons. Bliss is ready to spring from the edge, shouts *8–9–2–3–4–JUMP!* Voice and splash bounce off the cool tiled walls, and the sun is bright on the turquoise water. The class sings the "Hokey Pokey" and the "Wheels on the Bus," and when they are done with those he says, *More song, Mommy.* But class is over, and they must emerge from the pool. Mothers and children file off, their wet feet slapping the deck. In the echoing locker room, everyone showers in an open room, the easy roaming bodies of naked women and children together. Women lean their heads under the blare of hand dryers. They button oxford shirts and slip into leather penny loafers and hand their children snacks of saltines and bags of granola. The parking lot thrums with heat, and their cooled skin is still faint with chlorine. Click into the car seat, and on the way home, waiting at a stoplight, she sees in the rearview mirror her son has flopped his head into sleep.

SHE DIDN'T LOOK at anyone the way she looked at my brothers. She deemed kindergarten Duncan the kindest person she has had the luck to meet. Grown, he will send her money to supplement her social security checks, she predicts, and she is right. Her girls are studious and wound tight, like her. I begin to set an alarm clock with crayon hands in elementary school, and Katy, the night before first grade, not trusting even that fail-safe, sleeps in her first-day outfit. But the boys fascinate her with their difference. Bliss only yawns when my mother calls him by name each morning, and later still, after she has climbed the stairs to his room, stirs sleepily under the sheets when she shakes his shoulder to wake him. She shops for their size fourteen shoes, leans girlishly into their six-foot-plus frames. They are physically big and emotionally kind, and she had made them so, though she didn't entirely understand how.

She loved my father and my stepfather and some men in between, and I watched her love all of them bravely, without fear or restraint.

But after the divorce, I also watched from a magnolia tree while a family friend delivered sacks of groceries to our front door. Aside from a stint in a jewelry store while my father was in law school, my mother had never had a paid job in her adult life. This is also what comes from loving a man without fear or restraint.

I do not want to be made a fool of, I repeated in one romance after another, as if anyone were capable of assuring that but me.

"Oh, Sarah," my mother explained once I was married. "I wasn't a fool. That is a little girl's understanding of a grown woman's problem," she said. And: "I would do it all again."

What is a grown woman's understanding of a grown woman's problem?

That if I, too, am quick to fall in love, and I am, it is because of her. See: guileless; also: open, unguarded. It occurs to me loving this way may not be smart for a grown woman. Romantic love so often seems at odds with seriousness, and it does not endure. But what does? Why should duration equal significance? Besides, I know no other way. She would say there is no shame in relationship—in deep feeling, a surge of hormones, the pleasures of the body, she would say. Nor is there in its end.

"I never understood the term 'codependent,'" she said. "Isn't that the nature of being human, to depend on each other?"

OTHER FAMILIES we knew sent Christmas cards of a particular type—a studio portrait, each parent and child in coordinating ivory cashmere sweaters, a teenager with a wedge haircut, a hand positioned on a sister's shoulder to suggest love. Or a full-denim portrait, chambray shirts and 501s in the great outdoors, a tree swing for the youngest and everyone else's shiny boots and loafers buried in the colored leaves.

When our Christmas tree was decorated with miniature birds, strings of wooden red beads, classroom-crafted paper chains, and bubbling, multicolored lights, a photographer arrived for our own season's greetings. We sat on the burgundy velvet couch in the living room.

It started civil enough. Parents in the center with baby Bliss on our mother's lap, and the rest of us crowded around. I am in a six-year-old's perfect outfit: pigtails and pink tights bunched at my ankles above patent leather Mary Janes. Then Katy, already regal at eleven, her hair glossy and smile beguiling. Duncan's eyes look naughty beneath his thick wave of hair, but he is thirteen, and that is his job. Everyone in this picture has a different shade of red hair.

We can only hold it together for so long. Duncan cracks a joke and calls a kid rebellion. Then I'm splayed across my parents' laps screaming with laughter, my hands cupped around Bliss's smiling face, as if to remind him he's one of us, he's on our side. Katy sticks her tongue out at the camera, puts her thumbs in her ears. Duncan's legs spill off the couch. He cocks his head; the white collar of his striped polo shirt goes from flat and folded to rumpled. He is the leader of our loudmouthed mutiny. The photographer keeps snapping.

In the first of these photographs, my parents are laughing. These crazy kids. Then their faces become obscured by our mayhem, visible only from their laps down. The kids take control of the couch, the photo shoot, the picture's frame. We are cracking one another up, spurring one another on. It is four against two, and we are winning. This is us at our best, a wild and raucous team, stirred into a joyous mania. Peace on earth, good will to men.

I do not know if my mother mailed one of these pictures as our Christmas card that year. It would have been like her to see the charm of our madhouse and take pride in her delightful, expressive children—a mother's description. I cannot say for sure. But I do know she preserved what others may have called outtakes, that the series hung in the hallway in a large, poster-sized frame, and that the photos tell two stories unfolding alongside each other. Read from left to right and down the page, it is both a portrait of sibling unity and a prescient view of a family's unraveling.

THIS WAS THEIR recurring argument.

I would like you to defer to my judgment in most matters, he says.

I have only one precious life to live, she says, *and I shall make my own decisions.* She tries, at least.

Away from home, outside the domestic sphere, she liked the dynamic better. In Santa Fe for the weekend, both sick, they stayed in their room reading aloud from a best seller and gossiping about the characters. "Our noses were so runny that neither of us could be on top. It was very funny. It was very romantic."

I T IS THE BEGINNING of the end for their marriage, and the Brownie leader is at it again. When my mother pulls up to the curb, she learns I have entertained the troop during circle share with details of her latest marital dispute. The troop leader leans against the driver's side door and speaks to my mother through the open window. *I liked the part where you said he had been a jerk the entire year he turned forty,* she said, *and now it is your turn.*

T HE HOUSEKEEPER has been gone six weeks. Economy move. Someone is always home sick: chicken pox, strep throat, another chicken pox, stomach flu. The pharmacist greets her by name when she places the telephone orders for lice shampoo, Kaopectate, orange Triaminic. She puts on the *Dirty Dancing* CD when she vacuums and pops a chocolate cake in the oven to cheer everyone up. A father arrives to pick up his daughter who has come over to play, and he and my mother stand in the front hall amid wet bathing suits, a rocking horse, and a month's worth of unopened mail. This man is also a pediatrician. He says it looks like she'll be needing a penicillin shot soon. But she doesn't get sick, and when she next sees him, she is wearing blue jeans, the mail is still in stacks, and baby Bliss sits on her hip. He says she reminds him of something he learned early in his practice. *God didn't make mothers*, he says, *He made women. Whatever that means*, she thinks, annoyed. It is only later that week, perhaps, when the house is finally quiet, the dishwasher humming in the downstairs dark, her husband not yet home, and upstairs the kids are asleep or at least pretending. When she is finally in the soft light of her own bedroom with her hair brushed and her face clean, sinking into the down pillows with something to read, she arrives in a moment that is her own and not in relation to anything else—not a carpool, a nursing infant, nor a man she loves. She is self-contained, not only a woman but the sole measure of her own life.

H ER HUSBAND SAYS he has an ulcer. He says he is so worried about money he cannot sleep. He says they cannot afford a trip to London to celebrate her birthday.

His doctor tells him to get a hobby. He chooses calf roping and barrel racing and buys a $250,000 farm with a five-bedroom Victorian farmhouse in unsettled country far out of town. He cannot afford it, but he cannot resist. The house, he says, is his private getaway. He says she gave him the ulcer. She says, *I certainly am powerful, aren't I?*

He spends all of his time within the barbed-wire fencing of his new farm. It is a neglected place. The previous owners left behind a pony whose hooves have begun to curl up in the shape of elves' shoes. The terrain is rolling but treeless, the landscape an ill yellow. He forgets to come home for Christmas dinner.

She struggles through the ticktock of the lonely weeks just to make it to Friday mornings, when the kids are at school, and she leaves baby Bliss at the church nursery and goes to see the marriage counselor by herself. He is kind with his fragrant pipe and soft cognac leather chair, and he tells her he looks forward to their hour all week. He is her bright spot, too, so patient as she wonders aloud what is going on with her husband. Why she had to spend so much time wondering, I do not know, except that certain dreams are harder to wake from than others. She had nursed a desire for this family for more than twenty years, and that hope had rocked her into willful slumber.

SHE IS PROFOUNDLY uninterested in sex and thinks it a separate issue that she is very angry at her husband. Their bed has been their reliable return to each other, and without it, they must find other ways to communicate. They take a walk on the gray November sidewalks to sort themselves, and she begins to describe her inner life. Feeling is living, to her, she says. She has only just begun to speak. Can't they talk about literature or art instead, he asks. She has no idea why she married this man.

SOMETIMES HE WOULD come home late at night and in the dark tell her she did not know how to be a woman. The culprit in their marriage, he told her, was her mother. There are games men like to play, he said, and her mother had failed to teach them. I don't know what games he was talking about, since I didn't learn them either, but I do know some things about my grandmother. That she spent her adult life flirting through offices in pink lipstick and shift dresses. That when my brother-in-law met her, he told my sister he now understood oversexed to be a family trait on my mother's side. And that long before that, when my grandmother's beau went off to serve in the Air Force in his tailored green uniform, she gave him one last good time for the road and something to remember her by: a wallet-sized leather book filled with photographs of her own tame pinup poses. A skimming rayon dress, saddle shoes, a wide and knowing smile. *Hurry home, lover,* she wrote on the back of one; *Remember these lips . . .* on another, stamped with the red outline of her mouth. When he returned, they married, and when he died, she discovered the photographs still tucked inside the sleeve of the wallet he carried in his back pocket every day, and every night placed in the top drawer of his bureau as he undressed for bed.

SORTING THE LAUNDRY, my mother finds condoms in the pocket of my father's jeans. It is becoming difficult to find a good book to read when her own life has become such cliché-ridden trash.

WHEN SHE STOPPED nursing her final child, her breasts disappeared. The fullness she craved was draining from her life. Was it then, or long before, when her husband ceased to moan when she unbuttoned her blouse each evening? Was it then, or not long after, when she knew she would not have another child with him? She makes an appointment with a plastic surgeon and voices a vague concern about no longer feeling sexy. He gets it, he says, he is losing his hair. His hair doesn't matter, she says, and he says her breasts don't matter, either. They laugh at their lot, and he sends her home. Yet the facts remain: One year her husband boasts he knows how to make her come like a pet monkey, and the next he has left her alone in the soft evening light, aching with the embarrassment of her own unmet desire. The only pet monkey she knows is Curious George, who never does as his owner expects.

IT IS A RAINY SUNDAY afternoon, the first day in a long time her husband has stayed home from the office. It is the domestic witching hour. Nearly dinnertime, she has mashed potatoes on the stove, wet lettuce leaves in the sink, a chicken sputtering in the oven. They argue about a plastic video cassette holder my father has purchased at Woolworth's for the living room and which my mother deems hideous. (It is never about what it's about, a friend's mother will tell a group of us girls in college.) As he storms out, she is seized by a feral, vicious impulse. She follows him to the porch, and throws her hot tea on his starched shirt. She grabs his arm, and snaps her jaw shut on the wide bone. There is the sour, metallic taste of blood in her mouth. *Miss Sunday supper*, she snarls at him, *and never come back*. We do not regularly attend any church, so the ritual of this meal, in particular, matters. But he is already down the steps, and when his engine roars she is wilder still, racing through the house, ripping artwork she never liked from the walls. She gathers dirty socks and expensive, unused sports equipment, hauls his case files from the hallway, and dumps the whole heap of it on the wet porch. The oven timer beeps and beeps again. The phone rings. *Hey, baby*, he says. She cannot abide her own threat, and now she must race again: She collects his belongings from the porch and stuffs them in the hall closet. He takes his place at one end of the table, and she at hers. We bow our heads and say grace. Typically, the most reliable source of joy in her life is right here, when the glass salad bowl is passed around the table, and the children are loud and pouring milk from the cat-shaped jug, and either she or her husband— they take turns—winks down the length of the table at the other. That night we all eat dinner in miserable, utensil-scraping silence. She would say she acted childishly, but even her own children have never bitten someone in their rage.

W E HAD A STEREO with speakers the size of my Barbie Dreamhouse, and I remember Willie Nelson's plaintive timbre filling the house as my father carried me up the staircase to bed one night, softly singing "The Party's Over" into the shell of my ear.

She returned to the gynecologist when she felt her uterus was slipping out of her. The gynecologist said it was. A harder problem to solve: Her husband complained it was impossible to get enough attention from a woman with four children. The doctor told her she didn't have four children but five. Divorce him, he told her, and you'll have men climbing in your window at night. He blushed when he said this, and my mother thanked him for blushing.

The divorce didn't happen that way, but it did happen.

I LEARNED THE WORD "cunt" the night my mother ran into the street to scream at my father. They argued in the red taillights of his Cadillac, his girlfriend's hair hot-roller curly and blonde through the car window. David Koresh and the Branch Davidians were under siege in Waco. On the news and at school, people talked about "cults." The words sounded the same to me.

Y OU ARE JUST LIKE *your mother*, people say. They mean long-winded and loud mouthed, wide faced, charming in finer moments, obnoxious in others. Actually, I don't know what they mean, so one day I asked her.

"I'm sorry," she said. "I *hate* when people say I'm like my mother."

But the night after she died, it came up again. "You look just like your mother," her friend told me at the dinner table.

For a long time before she died, she no longer looked like herself. Late one night, I found her distraught in the living room, flipping through old photo albums.

"I wish there were more pictures of me," she said, crying.

When her friend says this, I know he is not only talking about our faces, but of something inexact and iterative—my echoed laugh, how my lipsticks also curl into the shape of a shepherd's hook, or the way I absentmindedly stand with my hands on my hips like an angry teacher.

"It's like she's still here," he said, putting his hand on my shoulder, looking as if he wanted to kiss me.

N OUR HOUSE growing up, my mother's bathroom had a wall of mirrors outlined by globe lights like a movie star's dressing room. She seemed to take her time getting ready to go out. She might slick her lashes with mascara, then lean back, read a few pages of a novel, and smoke a cigarette in her long ivory robe. It had a ruffle at the neckline. Hot rollers, lipstick, the crossing and uncrossing of her legs. There were purple spots on them, small ones like starbursts, and thick, raised veins that looked like knotted shoelaces trapped beneath the skin.

The morning after a party. "I looked so beautiful last night," she said.

I was six, eating cereal. "How did you know?"

She looked pleased as she lifted the kettle off the burner and poured boiling water over a tea bag. "I could see it in the mirror, and in other people's eyes," she said.

THE MOTHER-APPROVED facts as she reported them to me, the ones her mother had not told her:

You are so beautiful, so intelligent, and so talented.

And: *Someone will always be more beautiful, more intelligent, more talented.*

And: *Someone will always be less so, too.*

"I think the healthily vain woman looks at her bare, God-given physical self, accepts it, shows her love for herself by making the most of her best features, and then gets on with living."

So let's get on with it—the rest of the story, every tangible desire these two women can have.

THE U-HAUL STOOD in the morning shadows cast by the twin trees outside our house. My mother's ring had been pawned. The expensive rugs, the green felt-covered pool table, the Irish wake table with a slab down the center as wide as a casket—all sold. Inside the moving truck were the basics: beds, sofas covered in blue and white ticking with spare white slipcovers, the Crock-Pot, our clothes.

A stranger stood bowlegged in our driveway, squinting in the June sun and chewing tobacco. Doyle owed my mother's friend a favor. It must have been a big one, since paying up required driving a forty-three-year-old woman and two children, five and ten, from Texas to Massachusetts. My mother let Duncan and Katy, both teenagers, stay in Dallas for the summer. Doyle could be trusted with what valuables remained.

He was a painter but moved art for money. He wore a stiff white cowboy hat. From the iron-creased legs of his Wranglers emerged the pointed toes of snakeskin boots. My father said *Howdy, pardner* in the country and to certain folks downtown, but I had never seen a real cowboy, and the only adult I knew who called herself an artist was Lindsey Russell's mom. Everything about Doyle was an enigma.

He pulled the sliding metal door at the back of the truck down like he was closing up shop. The four of us slid onto the seat of the cab, Bliss and me in the middle, my mother by the window. We pulled away from the curb with the nose of the truck pointed north, and behind us, my mother's white Ford Taurus dangling from the back hitch like a figure standing at the railing of a caboose.

Doyle switched the radio on, traveling the analog dial from one end to another. Country music, static, off again. I asked if we could turn the air conditioner up. When the windows were down, the humidity was like another body crowding us. Bliss slid off the hot black plastic bench seat into the roomy dark of the floorboards. By my mother's sandaled feet and red-painted toenails, his Power Rangers argued heatedly back and forth before crashing into each other until someone toppled. Bliss made an explosive sound.

We reached the state line. Texarkana is perhaps best known for a 1946 serial killer who struck couples parked on lovers lanes. But I knew "Texarkana" as a word I heard my father use on the telephone when he talked about his cases—the literalness of the place caught in my ear like a dumb tune. Where are we? Half here, half there, and nowhere soon.

When we passed the birthplace of our new president, my mother and Doyle got to talking. Three hours in she still looked fresh, leaning her elbow next to the window of the sunbaked door, her red lipstick polished and the collar popped on her lavender polo shirt. She, for one, didn't see Clinton's sex appeal, she said. She'd met him at a campaign fund-raiser and found him red and sweaty. It was Al who was the real charmer, she said.

Doyle laughed and pushed the gearshift forward, as long and black as a fire poker. The muscles in his forearms twitched. I had a yellow sports Walkman in my lap and the gray foam-lined headphones nestled on my ears. It looked like I was listening to REM's *Out of Time*, but I had not hit play.

In Tennessee, stopped at a gas station, the papers in the wire racks by the cash registers all said Conway Twitty had died. His hair was stiff and tall, as out of fashion as his name, I thought, with Elvis's pomp but not at all handsome. Still, I was curious. I asked my mother to buy a copy.

Doyle stood at the open driver's side door with the creased map spread on his seat. His finger traced a line along the bottom of the state as he suggested something to my mother. *That sounds good*, she said, smiling. He refolded the map the right way, and my mother said I could have the window seat. They talked about the man who died and a woman he sang duets with. It was as if I'd entered a room to find people cleaning up after a party I wasn't invited to.

I had never seen a state like Tennessee. Even the long, flat stretches of interstate did not bore me, the medians flooded with yellow wildflowers. Texas in summer dries up like an insect husk, but Tennessee sighed its green warmth into the cab. I was quiet and daydreaming. One day I would be grown and decide things for myself. Tennessee was my favorite state so far.

Late that afternoon, stopped at a brown, sun-bleak motel set in long afternoon shadows, my mother made tea in our room with her electric kettle while I sat alone on the edge of the turquoise pool, my feet dangling in. I so seldom felt weightless. The cement radiated the day's heat through the seat of my shorts and on the backs of my legs. The tabloid was open beside me, and I was rapt with Conway Twitty and Loretta Lynn. Events of love and death were to me still sensation.

It did not seem worth the trouble to change into my bathing suit only to swim alone. As much as I longed for solo girlhood adventures—I wanted to feel for myself the same independent pride I had for my favorite storybook heroines—at that time, I knew "alone" as an expression mostly of "forgotten" and also sometimes of "fear."

My mother and Doyle must have decided we weren't in much of a hurry. We took the scenic route through the Smokys, the truck chugging up curvy roads that hugged the mountainsides. Clouds draped over the soft peaks, and we barreled in like children pushing through the back of a wardrobe.

We stopped at McDonald's.

"I want a chef's salad," I said. My mother looked into my face, disapproving.

"It's too much," she said. I didn't know if she was talking about money or the amount of food.

We sat in a booth by a window that looked out onto an empty parking lot. Bliss wore his Batman cape and handed my mother the toy from his Happy Meal. She opened the pouch and passed back the Joker and his purple roadster and kept talking with Doyle about *Lonesome Dove*. There was never an arc of quiet between the last word of her sentence and the first of his. I squeezed a packet of ranch dressing across the top of my salad in a zigzag. I thought this was how to get thin. Walking home at the end of the school year in my favorite lavender shorts, a boy I liked yelled "redwood thighs" up the street at me so everyone could hear. I loved trees, but I did not love that. Lunch seemed to last a long time. I ate each stick of ham, each piece of cheese, the gray-yolked hard-boiled egg.

Each night we stopped at a single-story highway motel standing in the shadow of an overpass, the kind of place that cost thirty-nine dollars a night. The door to our room would spill into a parking lot. Did we only ever get one room? If the other bed was for Doyle, I never saw him in it. Mom, Bliss, and I lined

up in one bed. I slept in a t-shirt that hung to my knees, and my
mother wore her vanilla robe. Each night, she leaned against the
headboard and raked an orange-paddled brush across her scalp.
It pulled her loose curls into highlighted waves in the lamplight.
The television hummed until sleep, laugh tracks and sitcom families seated close around a kitchen table. In the mornings, I opened
my eyes to see Doyle silhouetted before the slats of the plastic
blinds. The whole room was blue, his legs lean inside his starched
jeans. His boots were already on.

Virginia, Maryland, Pennsylvania, New York. They dis-
cussed one book after another. *Sophie's Choice, A Bed by the Window, Anna Karenina, Beyond the Bedroom Wall*. On I-95, *The Prince of
Tides* sounded dark and thrilling. "What happened?" I asked. My
mother shooed me out of the conversation. "It's not age appropri-
ate," she said. Doyle looked at me with *Sorry, kid* sympathy, then
continued with my mother. He had a red mustache, thick as a
shortbread cookie.

I stared back out the window, pretending I wasn't watching
myself in the side-view mirror. My face was round and ruddy,
with a bob that fell to my chin and along my soft jawline. But
my lips had a dark natural stain, noticeable enough that a teacher
hissed at me in assembly to wipe off my lipstick. Along with red
hair, it was what I had going for me. It wasn't much.

I counted billboards. Dollywood, divorce lawyers, injury
lawyers, reminders from God, adoption hotlines, caverns ahead,
country buffets now with salad bar. I hadn't seen an armadillo
since Arkansas but at night I loved the way the sharp smell of
skunk entered through the air vents, shaking my senses awake
like smelling salts. I didn't want to miss anything. I saw a Volks-

wagen Beetle and punched Bliss in the arm. *Slug bug red*, I said.
Slug bug white. The interstate traveled alongside oak forests and
hardwood pine, black fences and paddocks with horses swishing
their tails at glossy hindquarters. Branches of flowering dogwood
reached toward the truck like an outstretched hand.

In five days we crossed the country and arrived in another world.
It was cool in the valley when we pulled into the driveway of my
grandmother's farm. Though the house was large, there was little
room for us. Nanny had her hair done once a week on Spring
Street, went to the Stop and Shop on Tuesdays, and said to keep
our showers to three minutes. My uncle, who was brown from
the haying, looked as if it pained the muscles in his face to smile
at us. Doyle stacked our belongings in the fragrant barn, filling
an empty stall where milk cows once slept. My grandmother
cooked Italian sausages, tomatoes, and green peppers in a skillet,
and we ate together at the kitchen table. The downstairs windows
were open, and I wished I knew where my sweatshirt was packed.
The air smelled mellow and green. We finished dinner in time
for Nanny to watch *Dr. Quinn, Medicine Woman.* I lay on the deep
carpet, sneaking one foil-wrapped chocolate after another out of
a covered glass dish and reading *People.* On the cover, Shannen
Doherty stared me down in stonewashed jeans and a black bra,
a heavy cross hanging between her breasts. Her fiancé had filed
papers with a judge saying she was so violent he feared for his life.
That night, I slept with my mother in her childhood bedroom.
Her senior portrait still hung on the wall.

The next day my mother was driving Doyle to Boston, and

because his return flight to Texas did not leave until the following day, he would stay overnight in a hotel. *The round trip is really
too long for a single day*, my mother said. I saw her soft robe folded
at the mouth of her unzipped bag. She would spend the night in
Boston, too, she said.

I sat on the stairs and watched the familiar parade of my
mother walking from the kitchen to the car and back again. In
our house, I had stayed in front of the television while Duncan
left for pool halls. He returned with his jean pockets filled with
rumpled twenty-dollar bills. When a car horn blared, Katy rushed
out to a silver LeSabre driven by a senior girl with the top down,
the words to "Roxanne" or "Red Red Wine" audible from inside.
Each time the door slammed shut, I stayed home. Now Doyle had
a knapsack over his shoulder, his hat on, and a thick hardcover
book in his hand.

"I dog-eared it," he whispered, pushing the book across the
step like he was passing me a note in class. "Don't tell your mom."
I wrapped my arms around his neck. His whiskers were rough on
my cheek.

The car engine turned over, and I watched from the window as my mother and Doyle pulled onto the smooth blacktop
of Sloan Road, edged in cattails and Queen Anne's lace and black-
eyed Susans. At the foot of the stairs, I split the book open on my
lap to the single marked page of *The Prince of Tides*. The plastic
library cover made a cellophane crinkle. Reading, I felt hot, panicked. My Barbie was having sex with Ken, but this was different.
My eyes couldn't follow the lines fast enough, and when I finished
the scene, I read it again. Did I want it to stop or to go on? I wasn't
sure. All summer sounds—the low metallic rumble of my uncle's

tractor in the field, the gentle movement of the curtains, their pompoms bumping softly against the windowsill in the breeze, George Jones's coaxing voice spilling out of the clock radio above the kitchen sink—all seemed suddenly vacuumed from the world. I was in on a secret I had wanted to know, and now I wanted to unknow it. That there was sex and then there was something else, and a man could wreck me in ways I hadn't even known. A man could wreck anyone. I wanted to be noticed, but I didn't want this.

My mother returned from Boston the next day, breezy.

THE JOB INTERVIEW parade required a costume for someplace darker, colder, fancier than home: sheer black stockings, low-heeled patent leather pumps, and a purple blazer with gold buttons. She returned in the evenings without the optimistic smile. I would live on white rice for a year, I said, if we could just move out of Nanny's. We were both determined.

With her first paycheck, we rented a little yellow house in town on Sabin Drive. It was a triumph. I slept in my own bedroom and liked to sit outside under the shady tree boughs that edged the property, brittle brown pine needles poking through my jeans.

Then a boy dropped me off after the movies. We were "going out," or "going," as we had said in Texas. "This looks like a serial killer's house," he said, when his mother pulled into our driveway. That was the end of that sixth-grade romance.

Yet I couldn't unsee the paint peeling back from the white

stucco in thin curls like pencil shavings; the ragged weeds that edged the front walk and driveway; the garage that stood agape, serving the neighborhood an unmerciful view of paint cans, bicycles, homeless furniture we couldn't fit inside. The house itself was shaped like a trailer that had aspired to something more. Shame crept into our lives like algae bloom on a bay. The neighbors hated us, Nanny reported, and wondered whether they should call the police when Katy and I screamed at each other. Somehow I had only noticed the crab apple tree in the front yard with a rough, weathered rope swing, and how I could ride my bike to the library on Main Street, or walk to the end of our dead-end street, cut across a field, and arrive in the rear of the art museum. Free admission.

My mother was less free to roam. Her long commute crossed a mountain range and was even slower in the snow. She counseled troubled kids, and then in the evenings, there we were: the TV on, the spaghetti pot in the sink, the bottle of Wild Turkey missing. Duncan's cutting out pages from lingerie catalogs in the basement, and Katy's running up the phone bill in her room. Bliss plays video games, Sarah chronicles prepubescence in a pastel diary with lock and key. My mother slides out of her shoes and sleeps on a bed tucked into the uninsulated landing of the back stairs. We are crowded, and we are lonely.

She made lists for reassurance. Here's all we needed: a table with a chair for each family member, a bed for each of us, too. Bicycles for those who wanted them, library cards. Her signature extras: red geraniums on the windowsills, a blue and white teapot. A tiny, framed watercolor landscape arrived in the mail painted by Doyle. By this count, we were doing all right.

But by less material measure, I think if she had not had us, she would have laid down on that bed and never gotten up. I don't remember her eating or laughing or smiling during this time—I don't remember her much at all. Her presence moved through the house like a fog, appearing on Sunday nights in plastic containers filled with chicken Rice-A-Roni and steamed broccoli for us to reheat for dinner during the week, and in the unopened pack of toilet paper placed under the bathroom sink.

*P*OOR RICK, Nanny said. *Marrying a woman with four children.* He didn't see it that way, so I think that reveals something about Nanny.

My mother's first love, a man with the bearing of a country veterinarian, was about to become her second husband. It snowed so wildly the night before the wedding, guests traveling from across the state were unsure they would arrive in time for the morning ceremony. We woke to a world shimmering and white, the streets blanketed and still.

Her wedding suit was damask paisley in peacock blues and black with a soft velvet collar. Beneath the nip of her waist, the jacket flared into a peplum. She looked like a queen in her winter robes. I had wondered about her first wedding dress. She said it was green, but there were no photographs from the day she and my father eloped, and moths ravaged the gown until it was nothing but a fishing net.

She stood in the upstairs bathroom, fastening the clasp of her necklace. By this time, two years later, we had moved to a cheap, paper-thin house on Linden Street, but it had a staircase. *Women Who Run with the Wolves* lay on the linoleum floor between her low-heeled pumps and the toilet. The contents of other rooms were already packed inside brown moving boxes. After the wedding, we would drive south to Rick's farm in New Jersey. I could count four new schools in the past three years. "You ready?" my mother called to me across the hallway.

My future stepfather drove us to the South Williamstown Second Congregational Church, the place where he had met my mother thirty years before. He put down the visor to block the sun, and she leaned toward me in the backseat holding a wide gold band between her fingers.

Would I hand this to her when it was time to exchange the rings, she asked.

I inherited my father's sweaty hands, palms so wet they left damp spots on my notebook paper when I wrote. I was afraid the ring would slip from my fingers. I was also trying on preteen prickliness.

Why couldn't she ask Katy to do it, I said.

"Because I want you to," she said.

She didn't ask for much. She didn't ask me to stop skipping so many days of eighth grade or to wash the spaghetti pot or burn through less International Tasters Choice while I watched call-in romantic advice shows. She asked me to stop watching *Melrose Place*, to move with her again to another state, and to give her this ring so she could wed a man she loved, one who loved her almost as much as she loved us. A man eager to love all four of us to prove it.

I'm sure I sighed. But I slipped the band over my thumb and wrapped my slick fingers around it in a fist.

"Thank you," she said in triumph, as she twisted forward in her seat again and readjusted her seat belt.

We went to the chapel, we got married.

SPENT THE school day turning pages of *The Bell Jar* under my desk in algebra and feigning stomachaches so I could lie on the black vinyl bed in the nurse's office during lunch. She asked questions with answers that seemed self-evident, like how was I adjusting to my new school. My English teacher handed back my poetry, "I'm here for you!" written in cheerful, rounded script.

After school, my mother drove me home on Ferry Road, past the blind fork. The overcast March sky hung heavy overhead. She was chattering on, wearing a cobalt blue turtleneck with moth holes at the ribbed trim of the waistband. Her face was inside a double frame: the dark line of her high-necked sweater beneath her jaw, and the black rubber edging of the driver's side window outlining her profile like a Renaissance portrait. She had pink cheeks with large pores and teeth stained from nicotine and tea. Curls sprang loose around her face. At the time, I thought this was a moment in which I realized my mother was beautiful. I no longer think it is only that.

She had once told me my father said she was the kind of woman who tied her hair back with the rubber band from the morning newspaper. If that is true, I think it one of the keenest observations my father has ever made. In the car that day on the ride home from school, I looked at my mother, and she was in love again, like a teenager, like I would be in a few years with the boyfriend we would call Rattail at the dinner table. She was forty-six. She was planning her vegetable garden and ordering fruit trees for the area of the lawn she'd started calling her orchard and peony bulbs for the ditch by the septic tank. For the first time I saw: My mother was a girl, too.

spring

*T*ELL ME WHAT *you were like at my age*, I asked in college. When I called home, I could hear the television in the background. Every night, my mother and stepfather watched hours of news. He was a Republican and she was a Democrat, and they flipped between Fox News and MSNBC until he began to snore with the remote in his hand. I wanted to know if she'd been in love with the first person she slept with.

She found this a dumb question. "Of course," she said.

"What about the second person," I asked.

"Sarah," she said, weary of explaining the obvious. "Of *course* not."

First: a stone mason I met on my twenty-first birthday. There were some red flags. He was tangled up in a vague lawsuit with a former girlfriend, and had lost his sense of smell after an accident—I hesitated to call it brain damage—leading him to call and ask whether I would come over to smell his milk. Not a euphemism. But when he stood behind me in line at the movies, he rested his chin on the crown of my head and wrapped his body around me, draped and protective like a layer of chain mail. I introduced him to my mother when she visited in the spring. He was late to the coffee shop, and I thought he might not arrive. Then he burst in from the sunshine, and she saw the bright smile and blue collar body, too. I had omitted the questionable details. "He's very sexy," she said, nodding at me.

Before him there had been an almost first: a cowboy who worked the door at the bar. One night he led me from the white wicker loveseat on his front porch inside across creaky floors. He turned on no lamps, flipped no switches, and so it must have been the light from the streetlights or the neighbors or the moon, because our bodies cast shadows around the windowed room. The light navy. Tall and sleepy, he put one hand on each of my shoulders and turned me toward the mirror hanging from the linen closet door. *Look*, he said. I saw his face over my shoulder. Is this what a man is? He wanted to give me something, show me something. *Look*, he said again, and I did. My hair fell in waves past my shoulders, my skin pale as the ocean in the moonlight, feet bare on the moaning dark wood floors. I reached toward the hem of my dress, pulled it over my head, dropped it at my feet as if planting a flag.

The man I married was so like my father, everyone said. But that night, as I pulled my face away from the cowboy, I was so struck by surprise that I couldn't begin to entertain an insight. What does it mean if, in the dark, the shape of a man's face reminds you of your mother?

WHEN I WAS NINETEEN, the man who would become my husband sent three dozen roses to my dorm room with a card. "One dozen for your beauty, two for your charm, and three because they're late," it said. My birthday had been the day before, and the arrangement occupied half the floor between my room-mate's bed and mine. I called my sister. "What does it mean?" I asked, and we both scratched our heads, if not genuinely con-fused, then disbelieving.

He was my stepfather's nephew, a story I found romantic and he found humiliating. He begged me not to tell it at parties, pre-ferring a cagey, *We met through family friends.* Maybe I loved the story too much. How my stepfather had attended college in the town where my mother was a girl, how he was her aching high school crush, and years later, her first boyfriend. Had my mother not left a note on the meet-up bulletin board during his reunion weekend, *Rick: Call Allison,* how would my husband and I have met? Inside her happy ending was my own.

"I'm in love with your daughter," he told my mother when we began dating in earnest years after Rick's arrival.

"Which one?" she asked.

He was eight years older but believed in another generation's kind of manhood: to open doors and hold umbrellas, pick up checks, and order another round. In Paris we stood on a bridge, and he offered me a ring. What we had, he said, made him believe in God. I thought it was holy, too. For the first eight years, I took his arm and followed. It is little wonder he admitted at the end he preferred me at twenty-two.

REMEMBER THE BEGINNING, driving to a movie theater across a state line on a flat stretch of highway. The day was overcast with hot July haze. He leaned back into his seat with one hand on the wheel and the other firm on the gear shift. I thought that was silly; it was an automatic transmission. I also thought, as our silent car passed the Chevron station on the left and overgrown farmland on the right, that this trip would unfold in quiet. Around this time, I began asking with semiregularity, *What if we run out of things to talk about?* He found this question kind of cute, I think. Didn't it show how much I was trying? For me, the idea arrived in the car like a bill in the mailbox, the sort you stuff in a drawer and decide to deal with later.

But I cannot omit another memory, likely from the same week, sweeter and as significant in my mind, the one that made more impact at the time, the one that allowed everything to follow. Independence Day. We walked in the early evening, and because we were new lovers, could not travel far beyond the first intersection before we stopped to embrace. There were no cars on the road and the hem of my skirt fluttered at my knees in the humid breeze. The sound of fireworks in the distance. Here, fireflies. I wanted to tie myself up in his arms and he wanted to be the rope.

We decided to walk on.

ONCE HEARD an anthropologist on the radio explain our brains awash in the hormones of sexual attraction. "Love is madness," she said. "You're *literally* insane."

So there's that excuse.

O NCE, MY HUSBAND helped me carry sixteen volumes of the Time-Life *Foods of the World* series from a church jumble sale on the Upper East Side home to our apartment in Brooklyn. He was very romantic.

At my first job in New York, I stood at a photocopier for hours, staring blankly at the gray cubicle walls of a morgue-quiet academic press. I moved manuscripts from one pile to another, sent the same letter. Congratulations so-and-so, herewith find a contract, a very small check, your modest dreams coming true.

After bills each month, $160. If I called my mother crying from a bench in Madison Square Park, which was not uncommon, she told me I needed more vitamin D. "Go outside and stare directly into the sun," she urged, advice I regretfully followed.

Things were better at home when a chicken roasted in the oven or eggs cooked in a hot buttered pan, even better when my job became food editor. Cooking was a meditation, I thought. It anchored me in my body—here was my hand, holding a knife, slicing through celery. Here I was, standing on the black and white kitchen tile of my first apartment in Brooklyn, listening to records, making dinner. Here I was, I thought, *living*.

It is a lot of meaning for a meal to bear, a habit I would not break.

W E WERE ALREADY falling out of love when my husband and I met downtown for a friend's book party. She stood on stage in a tight black dress and read from her memoir, and my husband and I drank champagne at the bar with her fiancé, listening. He turned to us as the room began to clap. "She is the most amazing person I know," he said, his face bright with admiration. I sipped my drink.

Later that evening, my husband and I stood on the dark Thompson Street sidewalk, waiting for a table at a sushi restaurant he'd wanted to take me to since we first started dating. We were finally getting around to some things, and still not getting around to others.

"Who is the most amazing person you know?" I asked. At the time, I did not realize it was a test. His face, which I never stopped finding so handsome, was illuminated in a streetlight.

"Your mother," he answered. "Who is the most amazing person you know?"

"Same," I said. That was not one of our irreconcilable differences.

I ASKED MY MOTHER if she believed in God.

"People are my church," she said.

BUDDHISTS SAY when someone close to us is dying, the veil that separates the living from the dead is lifted. We exist in full awareness of the end. Some experience this as pressure, like a deadline. *Now is the time to start living!* In later months, I would sense an urgency, but I felt it first as a space, like a window thrown open and then a breeze through the bedroom.

"It's very clarifying," my mother said.

My soon-husband was fond of the yearlong increment. On the other side of that period of limbo our real lives would start, next year, when everything would be different, most certainly better. By then he would be rich, he said, and we could begin our lives in earnest. We kept a cartoon he had drawn on a sheet of printer paper affixed to our refrigerator with a magnet. Drawn in black marker, there was a house with a kitchen island, a cock-eared dog in the yard, a nearby main street with a yoga studio, and at the foot of a staircase a basket, out of which peeped two tiny feet. Why such modest desires required millions of dollars wasn't entirely clear. It did not occur to me the holdup on our hands was not a matter of money or of time but of willingness.

What I understand now is that I was very young, that time was still to me a resource that was abundant, heaped around me like playground sand piles to scale, slide down, and conquer again.

That is why I could then still have more conviction in someone else's dreams than my own.

When my mother was sick, I began to realize the future would never arrive. There was no golden door we stepped through into serene forever. Time swept by us, more sinkhole than ascension; meanwhile, we never arrived there. We were always only ever *here*.

This was our ongoing argument:

Happiness tomorrow requires suffering today, he said.

But all we ever have is today, I said.

Somewhere in the middle was someone who was right.

"Don't take anything for granted," my mother said, and I groaned. "That's so *hard*."

"Enjoy," she said. "It's the same thing."

I WAS TWENTY the year my mother taught me how to roast a chicken. It was the deep dark of January, and we cut celery side by side on soapstone counters. She softened stale bread with warm chicken broth, gathered the torn cubes up by the handful and stuffed the cavity. I stood next to her taking notes, wrote *Bell's Seasoning*. I was about to move into my first apartment twelve hundred miles away and four blocks from my Saint Paul college campus, and this was my home economics crash course.

We baked a loaf of whole wheat bread that night from a stained page of the spiral-bound *More-with-Less Cookbook*, written by Mennonite missionaries in the 1970s. It was filled with her

backward checkmarks and a note to add buttermilk to the refrigerator bran muffins. She gave me its lessons in shorthand.

This is how to rub two pennies together and eat for a week.
Serve some of the chicken hot from the oven with steamed broccoli and a spoonful of stuffing. Pull the meat from the bones
and chop. Tomorrow, pile chicken on slices of homemade bread
with mayonnaise, salt, and pepper. Cover the carcass with water,
and boil the bones for soup. She took the bread from the oven,
knocked the top crusts, and told me to listen for a hollow sound.

We sliced two slabs of bread from the loaf, buttered them,
and ate the chicken and the soft, herby stuffing at the kitchen
table beside the bay window blooming with tall amaryllis and
paperwhite bulbs. She wrote a grocery list. Here's what to keep
in your pantry. She wrote Bell's Seasoning, too. Here's how to
soften brown sugar. Here's how to make a cheap chocolate cake
in a sheet pan, and here's how to cover it with walnuts so no one
sees its uneven surface. She ripped the list from a pad, folded it,
and sent me back to Minnesota for the spring semester feeling
equipped as a pioneer.

Once there, in my sunny kitchen, I followed her instructions
and hatched herb seedlings in empty eggshells on the sill of the
kitchen window next to the table where I read Richard III. My room-
mates entered the kitchen, sniffing. Something rotting, they said.

WE TREATED HER first illness as a blip. It was fall, and my
siblings and I took turns joining our mother at a New Jer-

sey hospital every other Friday. Under a mobile of one thousand paper cranes, we sat in a ring of recliners we called the "chemo corral." We had jokes for everything. The nurses handed her tea in paper cups while Tamoxifen entered her body through a port beneath her collarbone. She wore a short strand of gold beads, dented from teething babies and taken, she claimed, off the body of a dead relative. I sat beside her with a laptop scrolling through china patterns. My wedding would be the following October. We laughed too loudly about things I can't remember, until the nurses returned, their hands tea-less this time. *Some people here are really sick*, they scolded.

But we were not them. Her children love chemotherapy, she joked to the staff. It was the only time we could claim her undivided attention. None of us realized how bad she looked until we saw the photographs after Thanksgiving. In the kitchen, reaching toward a guest's newborn, her expression is joyous but her skin colorless. Her body was vanishing as if in a film dissolve. I missed her eyebrows. She missed them, too.

After the holidays was radiation, and after radiation was remission. By the time her peonies bloomed in June, she and my stepdad were planning a trip to Scotland. It's so nice to take you for granted again, I joked on the phone. In October, wearing a red silk shantung suit, she hooked her arm through my left elbow and walked me down the aisle.

NEARLY FIVE YEARS later, we were not granted the same luxury of disbelief. She had been dragging her right leg around for months, complaining of a yoga injury. By the time she entered the chemo corral just before the holiday season, she was one of the really sick ones. This cancer was not excisable; it was embedded in her bones, had burrowed its way into the marrow, nested in her soft organs. We didn't have as many jokes, so we embraced understatement. She was *sick*, we said.

I don't remember her losing her hair, only when it was suddenly gone. She wore scarves tied loosely around her bare scalp: botanical block prints on Indian cotton, batiks, and large silk squares she'd worn at her waist and neck in the 1980s. She wasn't very good at tying them. They were always gathered loosely, slipping off, and she'd tug them lower on her forehead. "At least I haven't lost my eyebrows this time," she'd say at the downstairs mirror, putting on lipstick.

She lost other things instead. Twenty-two pounds, her toenails, taste buds, nerve endings. My childhood had been measured in the width of her back. When we hugged, I'd run my hands inside the deep channel of her spine, her bones flanked on either side by dense muscle. She had rowed crew and run after four kids, arms loaded with laundry and plastic bags from Tom Thumb. Now, her body was a stranger's. Unable to stand upright, she curled over a walker. But I recognized her hands. Her fingers were long for the size of her palm, with freckles beneath the knots of her knuckles. They're the same as mine. She gripped the steering wheel at ten and two.

Driving, she said, was the only thing that made her feel normal, but even quick trips were disrupted by nausea. She would feel a wave rise in her throat, keep one hand on the wheel, and extend the other toward me. That was my signal. I reached for the roll of paper towels she kept on the floorboards, ripped off a wad of rough sheets, and thrust them toward her. It was like a gym class relay race. *Here!* She held them to her mouth like an oxygen mask, then clenched the wheel, staying straight. She looked down the double lines of the road like a gangplank and took deep, deliberate breaths. *I just, need, to relax.* Once, after she returned home from a meeting, I found her in the driveway wiping streaks of yellow vomit from the inside of the driver's-side door.

It was like science fiction. First, she shrank. Wearing new black corduroys in a size formerly unknown to her, her concave thighs left dead air between legs thin as a fashion model's. More jokes.

Then she grew, expanding in all the wrong places. She unbuttoned the new pants to accommodate the swell, and my sister and I, stopped under a traffic light, wondered aloud what was growing inside. Her blood vessels began to leak into the tissue, so that her upper arms swelled like Popeye. Then her calves, ankles, and feet. Sometimes the pressure of the fluid was so great it would burst the skin. She sat at a luncheon, her feet in a pool of herself.

Try not to lose any weight, the oncologist said. Not dying seemed like a matter of meals. To lose weight was to move into an unseen space, the way headlights round the walls of a room at night, illuminating it a final time before a car turns the corner.

Here's what I heard: If she eats, she'll live. My older brother had gotten into the habit of depositing protein shakes on the bottom shelf of her refrigerator. They accumulated there, untouched. I could do better, I thought.

I was thirty-one the June Saturday a friend drove me out to my mother's farm. I left my husband and the china we had finally settled on—paper-thin and plain white—in our Brooklyn apartment for the summer. It did not occur to me that what I did looked like leaving; I would return for meetings at work and for date nights, I said, and my stepfather could use the break. I packed a suitcase of summer dresses, a sharp knife, and my good sea salt. When we turned into my mother's driveway, the weeds in the garden were waist high, and the redbud in front of the house was split in half, pulled apart by the weight of its two heaviest branches. It did not occur to me I might fail at any of what I attempted to save. I arrived in my mother's blue and white farmhouse kitchen. I thought if I could cook, I could cure.

WROTE A NEW grocery list. No peanut butter, she told me, unless it's with saltines. Potato skins sounded good and those sticks of cheddar cheese wrapped in plastic she could stick in her purse. Hamburgers, devil's food cake, creamy potato soup made with real cream. Crisp toast with salty butter, Greek yogurt, guacamole. She liked fish still, she said, and steak, and grease-stained sacks of fried chicken from the grocery store. Salads—big piles of ribby romaine, bright with vinegar. She had dressed one most nights for the past forty years. Now it was my turn.

We shopped together when she felt well enough, but when

her feet ached from neuropathy, and shoes seemed only to make it worse, she walked into the Amish market wearing thick wool socks. Waiting in line for a pretzel-wrapped sausage to share, another woman, about my age and tight with propriety, stared at my mother's feet as if a barnyard animal had clod into her dining room. My mother didn't notice; she was watching the bonneted women braid dough before dropping the pretzels into fryers of hot oil. The woman standing with us in line had a child with her, one who kicked his chubby legs from the top shelf of the shopping cart. She was ordering a platter for a party, sighing and shifting from one foot to another, impatient with the wait, and annoyed that a bald woman and her bitchy daughter were now standing in the way, foreshortening her view.

My rage was stealth. Its arrival never surprised me since I could feel it there, quiet but ever present in my body, like the steady machinations of menstruation. Still, it was startling when it ruptured the surface of an ordinary day. Women riled me— generations of them who walked together arm in arm through the parking lot of the zoo, who posted photos from a bright hospital room where there were more eager arms than could hold a swaddled new baby. Or a woman like this one, one who I had deemed insufficiently pleased with her precious little life and the littler one she had made, one with so much ahead that she could blithely waste what was being wrenched from my fingers, one who I knew nothing about, and yet had seen enough of. She could feel my glare.

"Am I in your way or something?" she asked.

"Not at all," I said, my mouth lifting into the kind of smile I had learned watching women in Texas. "But I believe we were next."

I N DALLAS, I had accompanied my mother on mornings of endless errands. JoAnn Fabrics, Weir's Furniture, Snider Plaza. This
was the only bearable time to be outside in high summer—before
the heat of the day gathered thickness and the sun burned, relent-
less. East of the skyscrapers, where shotgun houses sat behind
parched lawns and hanging laundry, five aluminum structures
similar in dimensions to a football field rose from the colorless landscape. On their short sides, under the triangle of their
pitched roofs, each was painted with a number. I remember 4 and
5. Inside, parked pickups, flatbeds facing in, filled with watermel-
ons, with cantaloupes, with honeydew, trucked in from anonymous tracts of land in east Texas off I-35. This was the farmer's
market in the mid-1980s. No bluegrass band, no cooking demos,
no heritage pork.

The vendors were men. Tan and ropey thin, they tucked
soft packs of cigarettes into the chest pockets of their worn cotton shirts. They were polite but terse, wore mesh-backed base-
ball caps and mirrored sunglasses. My mother strode the length
of the buildings in blue jeans and square sunglasses with lenses
that faded to the palest purple. Her hot-roller curls were brushed
loose, her perfume deep as ripe melons. She pointed at quarts of
peaches and red plums, and the men tumped green cardboard
containers of fruit into plastic grocery sacks. She said something,
and they laughed. She hooked the bags over her forearm, took
her change, and we walked to the back of another man's truck
to buy tomatoes and corn. If there was a breeze that day, and my
hair were gathered into a ponytail, I could feel the air move at the
nape of my neck.

We began to run errands together again. A few rolling miles from her home with my stepfather, at the Dvoor dairy farmer's market on the Route 12 circle, my mother leaned on her walker, stooped like Nanny before she died. She was only sixty-three, but she moved like an old woman. I followed her around the circle of vendors. We bought sweet potatoes from a young farmer with short sleeves and a tan, easy smile. His looked great, she told him, what was his secret? His face brightened, and he explained the conditions were right this year, and how to keep them over the winter in a cool garage. He handed her change, and she pushed it in her pocket, raising her shoulder like a girl. She hooked the bags on the handles of her walker. We moved on, and she sighed. "I used to be cute," she said.

On our way to the car, a little boy ran up to my mother with a coffee can. "Would you like to give to the Hunterdon Land Trust?" he asked. She pulled a dollar from her pocket and slipped it in his can. The boy looked back at his own mother, who handed him a roll of stickers. "Say 'thank you,'" she urged. "Thank you!" he chanted, then peeled off a sticker and placed it on my mother's extended forefinger. She put it above her breast. "I give," it said.

She was tired, so I drove us home, stopping at the Texaco just as the gas light turned on. The attendant was young, and we smiled at each other. When he turned his back to lift the nozzle from the pump, my mother looked ahead through the windshield, delighted by something unseen.

"What?" I said.

"Only a beautiful young woman could buy ten dollars worth of gas at a full-service station," she said. "Enjoy it."

MY HUSBAND CALLED to say he'd been staying up all night writing code for his iPhone app and eating cold pizza for dinner. "That sounds grim," I said. "Life without my wife is grim," he said. On the weekends, he worked from bed with the curtains drawn. He thought he had Lyme disease, lupus, Celiac, a stomach parasite, cancer. The doctor told him to stop googling symptoms. I told him I could not hold all our joy.

I BUILT FOUR raised beds inside the fence of my mother's large garden. Some things, neglected, were still kicking: the apricot, apple, and plum trees; the raspberry bush. I ran the mower through the overgrown grass to cut a path, and then my mother rolled her walker out to talk me through the next steps before heading back to the porch to read the newspaper.

Inside the four-foot square beds, I made layers according to her instructions: newspapers and collapsed cardboard first to block weeds; then rotted sheep manure, shoveled from the heap as big as a jungle gym behind the barn; a six-inch crown of dark and fragrant soil.

We had ordered the seeds before the snow melted from catalogs with pen-and-ink illustrations, and my mother had drawn the beds to scale on graph paper. Now, I pushed the seeds into the soil with an unsure index finger. Basil, a mix of bitter Asian greens, Brandywine and Big Boy tomatoes, Cashflow summer squash and zebra-striped zucchini, bright French breakfast radishes, two kinds of kale. We had decided to devote an entire bed to flowers, for beauty and for the bees. The envelope of cosmos was called the Sensation Mix. The winter squash were space hogs, so my mother suggested piling the manure between the walls of two separate beds and planting them there, free-form.

It was too late in the season for any of this, and in my panic, I treated it more as science than art. I cut back and forth across the lawn to the porch to ask follow-up questions. My mother sat on the chipped wicker furniture repainted white each year before this one. I stood in front of her, sweaty and concerned about seed spacing. She was nearly subsumed by the slipcovered cushions and the sections of the paper on her lap, but she was calm in the hot, insect buzz of the afternoon.

"There's no way to screw this up," she said. "What's the worst thing that could happen?"

Within days the green tops of the radishes sprang right out of the dirt, and I dug them in wide-eyed marvel, before slicing them into salads I handed to her at lunch. I was amazed at how simple it was to grow something from seed.

I give.

HER YOUNGER BROTHER, Quennie, hosted a picnic at his dairy farm in Westminster, Vermont, pitching a party tent beside the driveway so we could linger for the afternoon out of the sun eating hamburgers and potato salad. One of my younger cousins had returned home with her newborn. Together with my sister's daughter, the babies rolled and toppled on a yellow blanket spread at my mother's feet. The skin hung loosely from her bony jaw, slipping from her face like a landslide. She wore a black daisy-print bucket hat someone had given her.

"I feel so happy, and so stimulated!" she said. She looked terrible.

I paced the rows of my aunt's gardens, then stepped out of sight into a shed. It smelled like hay and bicycle tires. I could hear my mother's laugh as the babies played with the Hungry Caterpillar, an orange rubber ball, a toy Hess truck.

I wanted to be pregnant, and I needed my husband's help. But the baby I wanted was not with him, it was with her. For her. Birth was the logical continuation of a circle, the reassurance to both of us that as she died, something of us grew. It was the closest I could come to knowing my mother from inside the vessel of my own skin, to understand how she loved, and to pass it on. This was my inheritance. These were the only riches I had ever cared about. *I give.*

But before I went to care for my mother, and again after I returned home, each month, timed perfectly to ovulation, my husband and I argued about something small, then walked into our bedroom stony and lay in the dark, silent and awake with our backs to each other, the way you do when there is a big thing no one is yet ready to say.

COOKED WHOLE sides of salmon with thick, fennel-flecked yogurt sauce. Outside, over charcoal's gray ash, I grilled but-terflied chicken and then pounded parsley and basil in a mortar before adding a stream of green olive oil. I carried glass jugs of full-fat chocolate milk home from a local dairy. I made a peach crumble and burned the top, then scooped ice cream to cover it. I assembled tomato sandwiches with thick layers of mayonnaise on gold-toasted sourdough, and criss-crossed slices of crisp, hot bacon on top. Every meat had a sauce, every meal a dessert.

My mother insisted she didn't care about food. In fact, she never had cared, would have happily sustained herself on but-tered toast and tea were it not for the hungry mouths of a family and the required ritual of a meal.

"Don't get your ego involved with cooking for me," she warned. But sometimes she requested seconds, and those nights sent me upstairs, fist-pumping in triumph. I would lie awake in bed under the glow-in-the-dark stars I had affixed to the ceiling in high school, brainstorming extra calories. Soft pats of butter into her bowls of rice, more olive oil poured onto the salad. I sent progress reports to my sister in Massachusetts. "I will be very, very surprised if she loses weight this week," I wrote.

ME, I ATE peanut butter and jelly sandwiches. Popcorn. Or I did not eat at all, strangely comforted by my stomach's sav-age growling. It was one of three times in my life I have lost my appetite, increasingly disinterested in my own meals as I focused on my cooking project for her.

For my mother, I turned on the stove. For my mother, I set the table. For my mother, I took the wineglasses from the cabinet, struck a match, lit the candles, cut zinnias and cosmos and collected them in an empty marmalade jar. My stepfather would leave us at the table to our talk. Those nights, neither of us must have cared about eating. Our desires were less tangible. There is one way to slow a story as it speeds toward its inevitable end, and that is to linger in the scene. There was no other purpose for a meal than this: for my mother and me to unfold our napkins in our laps and sit side by side until the sun sank behind the barn and I rose to clear our plates, empty or not, and switch on the overhead light so we could stay and stay and stay.

SOME DAYS, the medicine made her weird. She dozed sitting upright, out of it, and listened with her eyes closed. She was there—wearing a twin set, cup of milky tea in front of her on the coffee table—and also not there. She dipped in and out of conversation to smile at someone, and then, drugged and heavy-headed, rolled out again. She was like this one afternoon sitting next to me on the couch while I read a poem aloud, realizing too late what it was about. She blinked her eyes open. Our faces were very close, and we looked at each other—really *looked*, the way, I imagine, a portrait painter can see beyond the surface of a subject—the shape of an eye, the slope of a shoulder—to what is immaterial but plain. I was watching her body waste its way off the earth, a witness to the very simple process of disintegration. But the material world, the facts of its entropic systems, were complicated that day by what I saw. How could a thing be in the process of dying when I had never seen anything more alive? I know, from the way she looked back at me, she saw the same thing in me.

I T WAS NOT a reversal of roles. She did not become the child and I the parent. My care was her own mothering returned. I didn't fuss, wasn't precious. I made soup, mopped the floors.

"You are me," she said one night when I returned from a meeting in the city. "Taking out the garbage in your high heels."

"I can't make her comfortable the way you can," my sister told me on the telephone, and I felt I had been chosen.

I N THE EARLY evenings, I pushed the wheelbarrow and shoveled manure. One night in the bathroom, washing up before cooking, I saw sheep manure smeared on my cheekbone. I smiled hugely, proud. There was bright summer air in my chest, and my skin was salty with sweat.

But I felt, too, the reel of summer's speed and our slow progress in it. I didn't know the names for country things and forgot family stories. What was the tiny quick-headed bird with yellow tail feathers? How do I rotate the vegetables next year so they don't deplete the soil? Who was struck by lightning while driving a tractor, left witless with the teeth of his zippers fused? There were days when I felt thoroughly consumed by the work at hand, when picking wet strawberries and fetching the mail at the end of the long driveway and thinning the overgrown thicket of basil was enough to occupy my mind and body. Yet there was a sort of light in the early evenings, a kind I failed repeatedly to capture in photographs, that would bring my eye to the wider landscape. Its quality was by nature ephemeral and also sort of skittish, weaving its view out of my hands perhaps for my own good, as if the attempt to reduce splendor to a single small frame was to misinterpret its inherent scale. The faded hay wagon stood empty in the field across the road, and the sun illuminated the tree line until it dipped behind the green horizon. Our home here on the Delaware River sat on one hundred acres. There were another hundred acres and eight generations of stories on the farm my mother grew up on at the foot of Mt. Greylock. What I didn't learn would die with her.

The world was in such full bloom, we were wavering on the quick edge of a ripeness about to rot.

THE FARMHOUSE SLUMPED into the earth. I could manage the vegetable garden but not my mother's flower beds, too, now overgrown with weeds as tall as high school basketball players. Digging them up was a sweaty, cursing war. The downstairs toilet sank into the soft, warped wood floor. The garbage bin overflowed. Open, abandoned yogurt sat on the fridge shelf, overgrown with black spots. The ants were everywhere. I sprayed bleach on the countertops and threw out old jars of olives. I could not keep pace with the decay.

My mother had stayed in bed all day. I climbed the stairs to her room, which sat underneath the sharp, pitched angles of the roof, and stood in the doorway, not wanting to enter. The smell was sour and fetid. I was feeling mean.

"It smells bad in here," I said. She looked up from her magazine, stunned, embarrassment and surprise on her face.

"You're rude," she said. "Maybe it's because I've been sick for eight months," she added, as if we were talking about the flu. My heart beat hot with shame. And because she wanted me to leave, and because I wanted to, too, I turned back downstairs.

Ten months later, I looked for something in her bedroom. She was no longer stretched atop the floral sheets with *The New Yorker,* but the smell was still there. It was from the dog bed, I realized, the thick mat of hair and oily skin rubbed into the plaid fabric and the rag rug beneath it, hot canine breath hanging close in the air.

A T NIGHT, crickets sawed outside the windows of my childhood bedroom, and I read sixteen years of old journals, turning their pages into the early morning hours, as if I did not know what would happen next. There I was, same as ever, a linked paper chain of self-replication, continuously through time, the very same shorthand for a simple, happy life: muffin tins, cross-country skis, a desk by an open window. When had I made everything so complicated?

Downstairs my mother was at the sink, washing dishes in yellow rubber gloves. My feet were bare. She leaned her hands on the counter and turned to me at the kitchen table.

"Can't you see yourself teaching English and having babies and inviting people over on Saturday night for dinner and dancing in the living room to the ukulele?" She looked at me, the plastic gloves drippy with soap suds, as if I were to answer. "Can't you see it?"

The yellow porch light brightened the window over the sink. Bugs circled the brass fixture outside. I could see it, I said.

"It's not too late to start over," she said. "You don't always have to be a good girl."

We spent the rest of the summer driving the long-way places, and when we arrived, sat in parking spaces with our seat belts on.

Maybe I should apply to graduate school.

Great.

I'm afraid I'll meet a man, and he'll pay attention to me, and I'll like it.

That would be the most natural thing in the world.

Should I start recording these conversations?

We're not saying anything interesting.

In our talk, we were not faced with an end. We were present and entertaining the possibility of something beyond, as if we were crouched on a riverbank, dipping a toy boat into the current.

"What if I expect too much of life?" I asked.

She shrugged. "So what if you do?"

STOOD AT the kitchen sink rinsing a colander full of cherries, black-red and glossy. My stepfather's car pulled into the driveway, returning from chemotherapy. The car doors opened, and my mother watched her steps on the uneven flagstones, or hung her head, I couldn't tell. Sleigh bells, sewn to a leather strap and hooked on the front door, rang merrily as she pulled the door closed behind her. She had a thing for Santa Claus, she joked. Jim Morrison and Saint Nick.

She declined a cup of tea. She wheeled her walker straight into the TV room. I poured the wet cherries in a bowl and followed.

She sat on the couch, her bony knees pressed tight together and between her slim thighs a widening space of nothing. I eased beside her and placed the cherries on her lap. She was already crying, and she did not often do that.

It was as if she confessed, the way she said it. Three pounds. Going, going, gone.

The afternoon sun was bright on her collection of terra-cotta pots filled with leggy geraniums. The leaves smelled like dirt. Her writing desk stood in the window cluttered with recipes torn from magazines and letters that needed response.

"It's very simple, Sarah," she said. "I love you, and I don't want to die."

There was nothing else to say. We each ate a cherry, then spit the pits into the blue and white bowl.

SHE WANTED A burger at the Stockton Inn. We sat on the front porch with a view of the bridge across the Delaware River to Pennsylvania. The traffic was very close. Silver-haired men rolled by in red cars with the tops down. Each had a woman as a passenger, usually wearing what seemed like too much makeup for a hot day. Motorcycles passed through the small town intersection with their guttural roar. I drank a gin and tonic. Did she have a drink, too? She'd sometimes order bourbon and ginger ale, which is what her father drank and her mother drank, too. The waitress seemed preoccupied and kept returning to our table to provide a forgotten menu, an omitted fork. Maybe she was new. Maybe she was heartbroken. I once absentmindedly wandered away from my shopping cart in the fabric section at Ikea to look at lamps. I returned to find the cart had stayed put but the purse inside it had not. I sat in the front of the store canceling credit cards and crying, because I was now not only heartbroken but also a fool. A man approached. "I've been looking all over for you," he said, "you walked off without your purse." I never got to tell my mother that story. She would have said, *See? There you go*, as if she'd known all along the outcome would include a good deed performed by a handsome stranger. This is one trickiness of grief. How can I "mourn" the "loss" of someone I can still summon? We ate our burgers and kept talking. The waitress refilled our water glasses, and a group of Italian men arrived, sat at the table beside us, ordered wine. They made a comment to my mother, and everyone laughed. The appliance store across the street was closed and washing machines stood in the darkened front windows like undressed mannequins. It was August, and the sun was low and golden, so it must have been around seven or eight o'clock when my mother said, "Who knows how many more summer evenings like this we'll get?"

fall

HOW ABOUT A last-ditch vacation? I had been asked to cover a food event in Hawaii, and we could make the most of it, I suggested. On the plane, most people looked like my husband: relaxed, happy, at least half Asian. The flight attendants walked up and down the aisles in maxi dresses printed with island blooms like Luau Barbie, then one leaned close to hand him his chocolate-covered macadamia nuts, and a sheet of glossy black hair fell around her face. He shared with me, 23A and B. I fished my fingers inside the slit of the shiny silver pouch and looked down at brown Colorado, rugged as a cowboy's calloused hand. The view gave me hope, as if I might be able to sort my life from cloud distance and then on island time. *Hawaii*, my husband had said in the days leading up to our trip. *Hawaii*, like an incantation. I looked at him now in his seat, munching macadamias pleasantly, engrossed in a game on his phone.

We lowered our heads for the front desk clerk at the hotel who draped long, muted necklaces strung with brown shells the size and shape of small beetles around our necks. Our room was seashell pale and sounded just the same, filled with orchids and a basket of exotic fruit. We stood at the railing of our balcony above two pools and countless palms, hushed by the curling ocean waves below. Who were all these people, I thought, reclining below us on chaises, lazily turning magazine pages and sipping rum. A thin strip of white shoreline stretched to Diamond Head, rising like a promise.

"Hideous," I joked.

He had been to this island before with another woman and here's what I knew about her: She was rich from her father's line of convenience stores and accordingly difficult; she had orgasmed most reliably with the light tickling of a feather, which she kept in her bed-stand drawer. I entered stage left on a romantic set piece. Blooms nestled on the crushed ice of a *mai tai*, the crisp bed linens in boxy rooms with windows pushed open to the ocean, the idle slide of slack-key guitars. New character, same motivation. *Birds do it, bees do it. Let's fall in love.* That evening we transformed into the strangers we had observed from our balcony. We ate plates of tuna soaked in inky soy and pushed aside the paper umbrellas in our drinks for a sip. Three men with ukuleles sang in swaying harmony while two hula dancers moved beside them. The women swirled their hands like conjurers, playing the air close at their hips like stringed instruments and then twirled their hands up into the darkness, smiling at some skyward beneficence, as if they could harness it from the atmosphere and tuck it back in their pockets. Maybe they could. "You would make an excellent hula dancer," my husband whispered to me. Later, my heels dangling from one hand, we walked the stretch of sand in front of our hotel. I stumbled ankle deep into the salty waves. That night we went to bed together in the dark, the balcony door open to the ocean sounds.

The sun felt like a menace, the way it bore down on us all day with its unrelenting intensity. I smeared my skin with SPF 70, sweat it off, reapplied. Pimples emerged. One of us was a natural to this climate, but it was not me. Beyond the Hard Rock Cafe and California Pizza Kitchen, the streets of Honolulu did not seem designed for pedestrians. We waited at streetlights for traffic to subside, then rushed across intersections without striped painted lines. Platters of hamburger patties and pork, with slices of orange cheese on top, ice cream scoops of white rice, everything covered in thick brown gravy. I wanted a vegetable. My husband had self-diagnosed a gluten allergy, and having forgone the macaroni salad, chatted merrily about his improved digestion as we ate at a plastic picnic table lacquered bright red beside a sun-dull road.

It was not hiking food, but we hiked. Pedestrians on their way to the Diamond Head trailhead must pass single file through a dark, narrow two-lane tunnel toward oncoming traffic, then across a parking lot where a truck sold shaved ice painted with syrups.

"How is it different from a snow cone again?" I asked.

The ice was finer, shaved, soft, he said.

The sun pressed down on us like a sandwich griddle while we wound through ochre dust and scrub brush on a cement trail. We drained our little bottles of Poland Spring. Halfway up our ascent, a woman had scrambled off the trail. She sat on the bald face of a short hill between two large boulders. She leaned between her knees to vomit. Her face was tear streaked. We stood below her on the trail, and I hollered.

"Are you okay?"

"Can we get you some water?" my husband added.

She raised her head from between her knees and stared at us with narrowed eyes.

"Please leave me alone."

So we climbed. My t-shirt was wet at my lower back, and the elastic of my underwear rubbed the crease of my thigh. My mind was scorched blank as the crater we climbed. The sun had ablated my consciousness. What was left was the wet rind of my body and a will that seemed to exist without volition; this is what moved me toward the top of the volcanic cone. Up 74 steps, up 99 more, then out of the sun to the final 43, enclosed in the tight spiral staircase of an old military observation deck. The task at hand was my imperative, but I understood the pull to rest between rocks, to give up before the payoff of the final view.

Here is what you see after the 560-foot ascent. Dry blond grasses that arch in the breeze; mesquite with brittle branches called *kiawe*; the crisp, long pods of *haole koa*, hanging like cicada husks from a tree; a red lighthouse on the shoreline that looks like an impostor; an abandoned bunker from the Fort Ruger days, salt bleached and battered, its squared shoulders huddled against the dull landscape and wind. More commanding is the wide view: the rising silver city and winding stretch of Waikiki, slim as the penciled eyebrow of a wizened barmaid beneath a distant domed sky. It is not just the sun that is unrelenting but the view itself— its insistent, bald-faced pronouncement, swaggering and unsubtle as a beauty queen. *Let's do it. Let's fall in love.* For a long time, we stood together at the railing of an observation deck, looking out. I wondered why I was so unmoved.

Good morning. There was coffee on the night table for me, a forehead kiss. My husband carried a plastic bag from the gift shop across the street filled with floral purchases. A blue polyester Hawaiian shirt for him, a rust-colored, one-size-fits-all dress for me. It was sweet, I could see that, but the color of the dress made me sad. It looked funereal, like late-season chrysanthemums.

"Do you like it?" he asked.

"I do, thank you." I got up from the bed to brush my teeth and pulled a cotton sundress from my suitcase.

"No, wear your new dress," he said, holding it out to me, limp in his hands. "I'll wear my shirt, too," he urged.

We walked the bright sidewalks of Kalakaua Avenue looking like employees on our lunch break in amusement park-issued costumes. A camera dangled from my husband's shoulder, and he stopped in front of a kiosk with a paper sign handwritten in black marker: WAIKIKI'S OLDEST LEI STAND 1928. The first owner's name was Kapela, somehow mangled into Aunty Bella; she had strung the garlands of fresh, fragile orchids by hand. Then her daughter took over, then a granddaughter. Such ephemera seemed expensive to me, but he insisted. He selected a pale lei of flowers whose essence, crushed and contained, comprised my favorite perfume.

He draped the ring of plumeria, tuberose, and gardenia across my bare shoulders and we kissed there on the groomed sidewalk of the Royal Hawaiian Center. A Japanese tourist took our picture. In it, my husband needs a haircut and I need sunglasses. I am squinting at the camera.

We had married in a boxwood-trimmed garden. He had not lifted a veil, though I knew he would have liked the drama of it; I wore a net at the crown of my head that cascaded to my waist like

Rapunzel's hair. On my way down the aisle, I had stumbled over
the uneven grass, and both my parents had gripped my elbows at
either side. The photographer caught my laugh, my young shoulders shrugging, my eyes in a half roll at my own lack of grace.
Nobody's perfect, my look says, though perhaps I expected others to
be. It did not occur to me to kiss my parents when the three of us
arrived before the groom standing between two large brass can-
delabras. When they dropped their arms, I stepped up to him like
a woman about to win her carnival prize. In the picture of us leaving the reception later that night, a friend said my husband looked
like the cat that ate the canary. Each of us thought we were the
lucky one. *I do*, he said, and back then, I did, too.

On our honeymoon in Mexico, I trotted out seven nights
of cheap polyester lingerie. Day three, emerging from the bathroom in the barest of all and bearing a beer. "Let's just watch TV,"
he said, putting an arm around me. I learned *mira* from dubbed
Woody Allen that night. *Look!*

We spent a day at Chichen Itza, where I carried a large black
umbrella to block the sun, like Mary Poppins on holiday. On the
way back to the hotel, after passing the bright, swinging hammocks
for sale by the side of the road woven by women and inmates, was
a vast *cenote*, an Indiana Jones swimming hole secret. The ceiling
of the cave arched over the opaque water like the dome of a cathedral with a light-flooded opening at its apex. Bats swooping. Someone took our photo there, too. In that one, my husband's hand on
his tanned hip bone, me in a red swimsuit, we look happy.

But before climbing into the van for the final leg of the return
trip to the hotel, he had slipped into a dry change of clothing.
Decades of swim practice made him adept at the deck change,

practiced perhaps more out of habit than modesty. Even at home, he wrapped a towel around his waist, stepped into his underwear and jeans, and then whipped the towel away to rub his hair dry, all without ever having revealed himself.

The windward side of the island was dense with water-thick rain forest foliage. In the rental car, my husband turned the radio to a pop station. I dangled my hand out the window on the highway, and examined my face in the side-view mirror. New pimples. We had three agenda items that day: visit a Buddhist temple; attend the Polynesian Cultural Center; and see the beach at Kailua, which he remembered from the last time he was on the island and in love with another woman.

We parked in a bleached, palm-lined lot, the sun-soaked pavement hot as a range, then walked a narrow sandy path past lush, low-growing sea lettuce and down to the waterline. I picked up a kalanchoe flower that had fallen onto the path and tucked it behind my ear.

The pale sand of Kailua Beach rings a turquoise bay, book-ended between the high volcanic peaks of the Ko'olau Range. The sky arches to the water, the convex curve of blue meeting blue and then our bare feet sliding into the hot sand. I wore a black string bikini under a white linen dress, the skirt made of widening tiers like a cake, swirling fiercely around my legs. His hair stood on end in the wind, his eyes squinting in the brightness. We walked up and down the beach, its beauty like an impenetrable wall. We never seemed to arrive. I looked for a break in the landscape, for a loophole, something set askew. The

sound of the wind at my ears was like traffic. I reached to rearrange the flower.

"Congratulations!" warbled through the wind to us. A man
with a naked torso, as tan as a nut, his hulking hand holding a black
ribbon leash that led to a perky Chihuahua, was beaming at us.

My husband shouted back, confused. "What's that?"

"I said, 'Congratulations!' You're in this long white dress, you
got the flower behind your left ear like a wedding band. And you,"
he looked at my husband knowingly, as if they shared a secret language. "You're newlyweds, right?"

We looked down at our clothes, and then back to him, laughing.

"Look at that," my husband said. "You're right."

Was that all it took? A plane ride, frozen drinks, a wide white
expanse of beach unspooling to the horizon? One of us thought
it did, more present in paradise than in our days making the bed,
clearing the table, rinsing the dishes in the sink. The other preferred the ordinary hours, felt here in the tropical sunshine as
empty as an abandoned shell.

The temple was set inside the deep shade at the foot of the Ko'olau
Mountains. I rang a peace bell, watched sparrows dive past the
lacquered Buddha, and then sat alone under a small red-roofed
pavilion. I counted my breaths, then kept breathing but forgot to
count. Then I started over.

People do not go to the Polynesian Cultural Center for the food.
We wandered through a cavernous dining room—an authentic

luau, someone boldly claimed—our brown plastic trays crowded with macaroni salad, roast pork, and tall red plastic cups with pellet ice and fruit punch. We sat across from each other. The long, communal tables were crowded with big groups of families. A kid spilled his milk and chairs scraped across the tile floors, echoing in a room loud with crying and benign talk.

Waiting for the big nighttime show, we sat in the grass near a tented pavilion that sold miniature ukuleles and magnets. It was getting dark. The tall lampposts lighting the cement pathways clicked on. Bugs swirled beneath them.

My husband began to tell me a story about the first time he'd been there. He pulled at the blades of grass while he talked. He was ten, he said. What he remembered was a couple sitting together on a bench. They had seemed hot and tired, but he watched them share a sexy glance, and then the woman shook her shoulders, side to side, he said, in a flirty little shimmy. He looked at me, sitting with my legs folded in the grass. "And now here I am, back here with my wife."

I was hot and tired, too, but I knew it was my cue. I grinned at him, then shimmied my shoulders in the pale lamplight. He smiled back at me widely.

But blackness seeped into the car on the way home, blowing in on the air off the ocean. The dark edges of roadside palms leaned over the highway like crouched, menacing animals. Salt and hibiscus through the windows. We named our favorite parts of the day. Me: lying on the stiff, shorn grass in my wet bathing suit after paddleboarding, the quiet of the temple. Him: postcard view at Kailua, fire dancers.

"It's funny," he said in the quiet. "Yours are so small."

"What do you think that means?" I asked.

"Isn't it obvious? You love the small moments, and I love the big ones."

"Yeah," I said. "But what do you think *that* means?" The dash of our tiny rental car gleamed blue in the dark, and the headlights only shone so far.

"I don't know," he said, kindly.

HOME AGAIN, Saturday morning, still wrapped in sheets. My husband placed a white paper cup of thick dark espresso and foamy milk in my hands. "Cappuccino," he said. I thought that the height of romance. My hair was a big red tumble, pink imprints of sheet creases on my skin and my eyes sleepy. "Thank you," I said, though my intention was to coo. He sat on the far side of the room by the window. I had asked my mother for a white slipcovered reading chair, but I never did read in it. The chair would be more at home in a nursery.

He asked if I'd had fun last night. It had been a late and boozy one with girlfriends. My head hurt. I suddenly remembered the bartender, the free drinks, his smiling, sidelong comments. I wanted my husband in bed beside me and considered the merest joke of competition might bring him close. At parties, I liked watching other women flirt with him at the punch bowl knowing he would come home with me. My efforts had the opposite effect.

"If you want to sleep with other people, it's okay with me," he said.

Maybe I should have brushed my teeth, my hair. That was our bed, the Tempur-Pedic we bought several winters ago when we had less money. In the gray showroom, we lay side by side on the mattress, our hands folded politely over our belly buttons. Then we deliberated the purchase at a French restaurant now long out of business. We decided to go for it, and I opened a store credit card that day. Zero percent interest.

What I was feeling from him now.

Later that day, walking home from yoga, I sat on a stoop and called my mother. Her voice wavered with rage through the phone, like hot air rising from a tarred road. It is so damaging to a woman's self-esteem, she said. If she wasn't crying yet, she sounded like she soon would. Her reaction surprised me, until I realized it was a remembered one. We were not talking about me, we were talking about her. The refusals, the late-night absence, the *Why-can't-you-be-more* criticism, the proverbial credit card receipt.

"No, no, no," I reassured her. "I don't think the problem is me." Maybe I should have.

I heard her surprise through the telephone.

"Oh," she said, and paused. "That's good."

THERE IS MORE to marriage than weekends and vacations, my mother said, and there was more to our marriage than that, too. But it was the time free from the numbing habits of our everyday—of commuting home, ordering Chinese, and then rinsing the plastic containers for the recycling bin—when the friction of our misalignments began to chafe.

He liked to argue in metaphor. After watching a miniseries on John Adams, he admired aloud the partnership of a woman like Abigail. Her endurance of long separations had been fortified, he said, by the knowledge her husband was achieving something great. I no longer thought my husband about to achieve anything great, and the part I remembered was the miscarriage Abigail suffered alone one summer.

We argued, recurringly and bizarrely, about a hypothetical road trip to the Grand Canyon. I longed for scenic byways and roadside slices of berry pie. Why stop at the world's largest ball of twine, he said, when we were on our way to one of the world's wonders. We should drive all night just to get there.

We were arguing about how to love. We were arguing about how to live. Then we were arguing about how to die, and in the end, not arguing in metaphor at all.

"You're in denial," my husband said. "You need to prepare for the fact that your mother is going to die."

I did not know how to prepare for her death other than to be witness to her life.

On Friday nights, when I boarded a bus at Port Authority and rode two hours into the Garden State, I watched strip malls thin into farmland. The evening sky changed over the countryside, streaked with clouds and color as the sun set. My mother and I sat at the table in her darkened kitchen.

She would not outlive her husband, she told me. She would not move into a condo by the ocean someday, or sew a slipcover for a loveseat in the tropical fabric she'd already selected. She would know only one grandchild. She would not, she said, grow old in the way she had imagined. She would not grow old at all.

"I need to be able to say these things to someone," she said, and so I listened.

I T WASN'T LIKE a plane going down. It was more like a car lurching forward, then stalling out. Each new chemotherapy drug brought a burst of wellness—deep reserves of energy, a renewed appetite. With it, she painted furniture, picked basil, whipped up a batch of pesto and froze it in ice cube trays. She knit baby blankets and hauled out the sewing machine. After she died, one of her friends mailed me two blue-and-white-striped Easter outfits. A seersucker dress and a seersucker onesie, both lined in plain white cotton. "Your mother sewed these for my kids," she wrote, "but I thought you should have them." She attended marathon board meetings and lunches with friends that stretched late into the afternoon. She would gain weight, take long drives, send long, chatty emails. We would all relax.

Each new drug also brought a spate of new side effects. Mouth sores, loss of appetite, nausea, peeling hands and feet, retained fluids, the full array of digestive problems.

There are only so many cancer drugs. The protocol was to try each drug for three months, then test to see whether there had been any change. There was a list we would soon exhaust.

"Rick and I were surprised to learn the results of my PET scan today," she wrote. We had been at this the better part of a year.

"I guess I should be impressed I feel so good when I have been pumped up with ineffective poisons for nine months."

Sometimes someone would tell me about a drug they thought was a "miracle," and I would send my mother a message. Was this on our list? Had she already tried it? And she would reply the next morning.

"It makes me very sad to think of my precious, luscious daughter reading about drug therapies. Pursue happiness, pleasure, and sensual delight! Cook, ride your bike, pick out your spring clothes. Just live harder! That is the medicine."

M Y BOSS ORGANIZED a dinner at an Italian restaurant in the East Village. In a private room behind heavy wood doors, my coworkers and I sat at a long table set under dim chandeliers. The cost of one night's privacy was one thousand dollars. Most of our tab was wine.

That night at the table, after the plates of squid ink risotto and sausage orecchiette had been cleared, when people began to escape outside to smoke cigarettes, when we were leaning back in our chairs having enjoyed ourselves and still draining the last of the wine, I remember someone began talking about wanting to lose weight. She pinched a handful of flesh above her waistband. There was murmured commiseration about thighs.

I had watched my mother age twenty years in the past six months, I said. We should enjoy our bodies. It's only downhill from here, and fast.

I must have been tedious company.

N MANY RELIGIONS and philosophical traditions, the body is an obstacle, a liability. It must be controlled or overcome, and to reach enlightenment, it must be transcended.

For years I practiced a form of yoga based on Tantric philosophy. I am not a scholar of Tantra, but here is what I understand. On Tantric paths, everything is sacred. Rocks, tonsils, an octopus. The human body itself can be a gateway to the divine. If it happens here in earthly life, it's called *jivanmukti*.

I cannot conceive of an enlightenment as a sustained state, static once achieved. But I have had moments of illumination as bright and flashing as a fish. They arrive unannounced, without fanfare—say, stepping off the Sixth Avenue bus or walking the foothills of the Blue Ridge Mountains. The sky turns lavender in the evening. Is that divine? I know it is the beauty of the material world, that I feel it in my body, and that it means something to me—that my breath will catch in my throat, that it fades almost as soon as it arrives, that I will be stunned again at its sudden reappearance.

THAT FALL I developed a new habit. Two blocks from our apartment was a storefront offering *qigong tui na*, a style of acupressure massage. Fifty dollars for sixty minutes. It was nothing fancy, but every week or two I returned to see a man who told me to call him Peter. He wore flowing black track pants, had broad shoulders and a wide, welcoming face. Sometimes when I swung the door open he was scooping rice out of a cooker under the low drop ceiling, but he would smile wordlessly, gesture toward one of the curtain doors, press play on the stereo, and I would undress in a bare room. It was always painful, the way he manipulated the tender knots tucked beneath my scapula with his elbow, or sunk his knuckles into the soft arch of my foot. I would allow myself to whimper, the face cradle growing damp, and he would whisper *Shhh*. When I returned to the waiting room, buttoned up again but also somehow undone, he would hand me a thin plastic cup of water and tilt his head with sympathy. I sat and slowly sipped, studying the charts near the register. They illustrated the meridian lines running through the body, how every area corresponded to another, and I would wonder about the original sources of all the hard places in me. When the cup was empty, I would sign the credit card slip and put on my coat. He would always stop me before I stepped back outside and give me one last adjustment. Pull my coat zipper higher beneath my chin or put both his hands on my upper arms and pat, as if warming me for the journey. And then, after several visits, he began to hug me, to fold me into his arms just as I was about to leave, and I would rest my head against him for a long, long moment. *Bye bye, thank you*, he said, and I would say thank you, too.

ONE OPTION FOR earliest memory: We have spent the day at the Highland Park Pool, where I lay my towel in the shade by the snack bar. Snow cones drenched in red and blue syrups, snack-sized bags of Fritos, hot dogs, the menu spelled out in black letters slid across rails like an abacus. My mother held on to the side of the pool, dutifully scissor kicking her legs and chatting with other mothers. Loud sounds of Marco Polo, the spring of the high board, the quiet pause, the punctuating splash.

In the hot late afternoon my mother drives us home on the tree-shaded streets by Turtle Creek in our red Suburban. I am sun weary, sinking into the scratchy gray upholstery, my limbs exhausted and the core of me cool from the water. It may be my favorite feeling in the world—the physical exhaustion after swimming that leads to a particular kind of hunger. It's when I most want fried chicken.

At home, I wriggle out of my wet swimsuit and pull a dry cotton t-shirt over my head. It hangs to my knees for sleeping. That evening, I sit on one of the two wide windowsills in my bedroom. They are painted white. It is the hour when the sun bathes the redbrick houses on our street gold. My window looks out over the top of the honeysuckle bush in our front yard. I watch as cars pull up to the stop sign at our corner and turn right or left toward home, toward Bubba's for biscuits and gravy, toward the Texaco around the corner to have their windshields washed, toward the evening bells ringing in the tower of the gray Methodist church. This is our neighborhood: Drexel Drive, Hillcrest Avenue, Mockingbird Lane. My mom has brought me chicken noodle soup, the kind from a red and white can, and because it was unusual to eat in my bedroom, this must be why I remember—how I ate it from frosted-opaque Tupperware, the noodles soft, the oil-splatched surface of the salty broth. It is the first time I can recall, with a certainty as indelible as bedrock, being within the envelope of my own skin. My senses surrounded my consciousness, vibrating like an electric fence. Outside my window, the whole world.

THE KINDS OF people who prefer to be naked, to stand at the kitchen counter fixing a sandwich in the nude, are still not dressed at their desk later, phoning the cable company. "I need to reeroticize my body," a friend told me on the telephone after her partner had grown accustomed to the sight of her long legs, bare and languid, draped about their apartment.

When the time finally came at the end of college, and I began to lie beside another body all night long, I was surprised at my own sexual ease. It was not because I believed my worth seated there, though I felt worthy of fun, desire, playfulness. What I cared about was meaning, and the pleasure of sex was another place it lived. It is mysterious to me, in the way faith can be. It seemed such a simple expression of self and an all-consuming act of presence, like a prayer, but one said in tandem.

I HAD NO male friends, no male coworkers. "You need more men in your life," my mother said. "They offer a different perspective." Maybe I would call up my old college roommate and ask if he wanted to get a beer.

"And you should try to smile at a man in the street every day," she added, like homework. This had never occurred to me. I had only ever been interested in the man whom I married, his hairline launching at me like an arrow.

In crosswalks and on the sidewalk, I let my eyes wander to bald heads and tattooed biceps. They were everywhere, and they looked back. I began to smile.

I F YOU WANT to understand partnership, take a dance class or go canoeing. *Hold me tighter*, I said on the dance floor. *Paddle when I say or just stop*, my husband instructed from the stern.

Sitting at a karaoke bar after Friday night swing, we once had a conversation we forgot to have before exchanging vows.

"Let's each write what our definition of marriage is," I said, handing him a stubby pencil and a song request slip.

I wrote: Marriage is physical and emotional intimacy.

He wrote: Life is a boxing ring, and marriage is my coach, wiping the blood from my face and squeezing cold water into my mouth.

Whatever that means.

T HE POLICE OFFICERS in line before me at 7-Eleven were buy-ing a day's worth of car snacks. Cellophane pouches and drinks were piled on the counter by the cash register, and one of the officers was still racked with indecision.

"Cheez-Its or Goldfish?" the one asked the other, who then looked at me.

"Go ahead," his partner said, waving me toward the cashier. "Slurpee's on me."

A week later, walking in Prospect Park, a squad car pulled beside me and rolled down the window. I worried I was in trouble, and then I recognized the face.

"How was the Slurpee," he asked.

It had been a very hot day, and it was great, and that was so nice, and thank you.

"I didn't know if you were married or what," he said, trailing off.

I wore a diamond ring and a gold band, but I don't think they ever look. Before stating what I thought the jewelry made obvious, I enjoyed the simple fun of that brief moment. A girl in a pair of wide 1940s-style shorts that fluttered in the hot breeze, a man in uniform, a summer day.

"Well, you have a beautiful smile," he said.

A FRIEND HOSTED a rooftop party. Guests wore feathers and eyeshadow and caftans. We drank dentist cups of whiskey, and my dear old friend introduced me to his new friends. After a toast, I called one of them a gorgeous man.

"Minnie, here, is a lady," my friend clarified.

Later, sitting on a low brick wall, a photographer touched my shoulder. He was a man. He asked if he could get me a beer from the ice chest, then told stories about midnight bourbons in Southern juke joints, about the pagans who pilgrimage to Stonehenge in spring and dance with wreaths of flowers, about a woman he once met at a trailhead who offered him a blow job when they reached a peak. I wondered how these stories usually went over. I wondered how it would feel to kiss him. But more so, especially in the days that followed, when I began to imagine myself at the end of a dark bar on a red stool, aglow in the light of a Wurlitzer, alone in another state, I wondered what it would feel like not to meet a man like this but to be him.

When he finally asked, I said I worked as a food editor at a big company.

"Oh," he said, looking at me as if I had just come into focus. "You're *corporate*."

I wish my friend had been on hand to intervene. "Sarah, here, is an artist."

All the terms were up for redefinition.

I N THE LATE FALL, on mornings when frozen dew still covered car windows, my husband and I rode together in taxis five long avenues to a basement office. For fifty minutes, before we each reported to work in midtown, we sat on a loveseat opposite a woman with close-clipped hair and long silken scarves, and talked about our feelings. *Permanent Partners* and *Goddesses in Everywoman* stood on her bookshelf.

The diagnosis was that we had very different levels of emotional fluency. After each session, we stood on the icy sidewalk with our arms around each other. Wasn't this trying? And if it was working, why didn't it feel better?

On the subway, I sealed myself up again, cordoned off the brief opening I'd allowed. At editorial meetings, when I was pitched stories about what rising lime prices would do to the cocktail and guacamole industries ("We'll call it 'Limepocalypse!'"), I did not want to look as though I had been crying.

"It will take fewer than ten sessions," my mother said. "Either way, you'll know."

It was exhausting, waiting for the final outcome of these two diagnoses.

That was when I began to fantasize about road trips, plotting giant circular routes around the perimeter of the United States. My escape was powered by one recurring daydream: My back on hard-packed sand beside a dying campfire under black cover of night, the fabric of desert sky pricked with white stars like cross-stitch. I would need a month; I would need a car.

"I get it," my brother, Bliss, said. "I ran all the way to China."

"Take two weeks," my boss said over vodka tonics. Then a few days later in the kitchenette, she suggested I could do it in one.

I applied to graduate school instead. I rented a hippie farmhouse upstate for a weekend to finish my applications. There was a portrait of JFK hanging on the porch next to a stack of firewood and a disco ball in the living room. The house was obstinately cold despite the fires I built in the wood stove. On the sheepskin rug, I read the love letter my husband had pressed into my hand at my departure. It was all too late. In the morning, I sat at the long kitchen table in fingerless gloves. I wrote about my mother. She was affecting my sense of time, and everything was beginning to seem urgent. Then I ran hilly country roads past Jewish summer camps for city kids, mixed myself a Manhattan, and cooked a dry-aged steak for dinner. When the fire died down, I threw on another log.

winter

GOOD ROAD TRIPS with a carful of friends begin with Diet Dr Pepper and beef jerky and an ironic Metallica lighter to replace what TSA took away. It was three days before New Year's Eve. While Laurie watched Chicago shrink in the rearview mirror, Jenny poured Sour Patch Kids into her open hand and cued up the lesbian soundtrack we've harmonized to since college. I sat on the backseat hump with one snow boot in each wheel bed and leaned forward between the front seats; I took the low parts. My husband was snug against his window reading the news on his phone.

Wisconsin welcomed us—a couple freshly in love and a couple falling out.

But we all loved the alien landscape. When the last glacier moved through the Upper Midwest, it scraped off mountaintops and rounded topographical edges, leaving green hill states that gently roll and unfold. The wedge of land where Wisconsin, Minnesota, Illinois, and Iowa lean their backs against each other was bypassed, so what remains is the Driftless—an area that is bony shouldered and dramatic with craggy rock faces and blind valleys. Insoluble limestone mountain ranges rise suddenly from grassy prairies, dark on the near horizon like a declaration that takes everyone by surprise.

The roads were snow streaked through the thinning towns.

Gays Mills got a laugh and was followed by Soldiers Grove, where all the lights were off. We turned left at the bend in County Road x-marked by a red mailbox and an old outhouse and slowly traveled an unmarked road past a snowed-over creek bed. It seemed like we were lost, like we had turned too soon and now overcommitted to our error. The car slid as we took a sharp turn and then, there it was on the left: a white farmhouse with a plume of wood smoke and every window bright. That was Annie's.

My husband lifted his bag from the trunk and cursed the cold under his breath. He brought his laptop but forgot to pack the long underwear I bought for our trip to Denmark the year before.

"There's no bad weather," I said, dragging my suitcase up the snowy drive. "Only bad clothing." I inherited know-it-all from my mother. He inherited long-suffering from his father.

That trip to Copenhagen had felt different, where we sat side by side at café tables with daytime candlelight and silver pots of winter heather. We drank strong, milky coffee until it was time to drink beer. First thing in the morning we were already off to a good start: I piled thick blankets over us in the dark hotel room and pretended we were prehistoric, bedding down under pelts of fur in the belly of a cave. Behind the closed door of the bathroom each day, I removed ovulation tests from my toiletries case. Walking the gray streets shopping for candlesticks and ceramics for our home, or on trains to see a cathedral out of town, I remembered what a good man my husband was. He bought presents for each of his coworkers, gave up his seat for women on the metro. I was very sorry I had forgotten. "What's your favorite part of vacation?" I asked, and he answered, "Seeing my wife so happy."

And now he had forgotten his long underwear.

"I made split pea soup," Annie said, while pointing to our bed-
rooms up steep, creaky stairs. She wore a plaid flannel nightgown,
waved her hand at the stove, and said help yourself. Jenny met
Annie singing in a square dance band in Chicago. In the city, Annie
owned her own business and wore lipstick. Then four hours away,
she lived a country life with a cherry orchard and shaggy white
horses in the paddock. She dug swimming holes and painted her
face with mud. The sign above the old toilet in her bathroom read
WHEN IT'S YELLOW, LET IT MELLOW. The simple things we drea-
med about, Annie made real.

She dropped the needle onto a Loretta Lynn record, and sat
back on the couch in the red glow of the Christmas tree. On the
Oriental rug, old beagle Betty crossed her paws like a lady, rested
her head on top, and sighed. There was a fire in the woodstove.

I was the first to climb the stairs to bed. Lying under wool
blankets, I heard my husband in the living room tell the story of
how we fell in love. It was the long version, the one he didn't tend
to tell, the one that begins with my mother. His voice traveled up
through the metal heating grate in the floor like a genie from a
bottle. It sounded like a fable from so long ago.

Jenny was wearing glasses and a topknot and meant business frying bacon and sausage patties. She pointed the spatula
toward the ceiling as she considered the larder, waiting like a
teacher at the chalkboard.

"We'll need black-eyed peas," she said, and I added that to the
grocery list, along with four dozen eggs, lemons for hot toddies,
tortilla chips. Laurie was out for a walk, but wanted to make her

egg-and-green chile casserole for breakfast and Jenny's favorite spinach dip; I added those ingredients, too. My husband was on the couch in the next room with his laptop. I brought him a cup of coffee.

"Do you want to go into town with us to get groceries?"

"No, thanks," he answered with a brusque smile. He stroked Betty with his bare foot. We were taking turns being optimistic.

The front door opened and Tommy stamped his snowy boots on the mat. He is as red bearded as a sea captain, and his cheeks were pink with cold from working in the high pasture. He knows everything Annie knows how to do, only now they do it together: curry burrs out of the horses' manes, repair the floor in the pole barn, shepherd the goats, build a one-room cabin. But Annie knows how to do things Tommy doesn't, like call a square dance and close real estate deals. *Who's that*, he asked of the woman leading a band of bolo ties in a tight dress at the lip of a Chicago stage, and that's how they fell in love.

"That smells really good, Jenny," Tommy said, and hung his snow-wet Carhartt overalls on a hook by the door. He sat at the kitchen table with a satisfied exhaustion. "Tonight might be a good night to fire up the sauna," he said, unfolding the paper, and Jenny and I agreed that it was.

After breakfast, Tommy headed back up to the pasture, and Jenny and I sat at the kitchen table drinking our coffee. We planned the day. After errands, there were country songs to sing, hills to ramble, tarot cards to read, dulcimers to pick at, beans to soak. We drank coffee until cocktail hour and bourbon until bedtime.

"Why are we so happy here?" I asked, as if there were more to it than the free expanse of vacation. It was sunny and bitter outside, and there were three swallows hopping on and off the bird feeder near the window.

"It's all our favorite things," she answered. "Maybe the question is Why do we insist on making our lives in the city?"

After a while, I asked if she thought they needed a new coffee shop in the nearby town, though I was tired of the sentence before it had finished leaving my mouth.

"Probably not," she said.

"How does anyone ever make any money without selling their soul?" I asked. She didn't have an answer for that, so we sat quietly for a few minutes, listening to the man in the next room, tapping at his keyboard, writing code.

In the evenings, Jenny and I took turns cooking. We kneaded dough for sheet-pan pizzas and heated old cast iron skillets until they shone. I showered coarse salt on thick ribeye steaks that hissed as I laid them in the pan. Annie sat at the table with her guitar and the three of us sang while we cooked. Stews simmered, root vegetables roasted, and breads rose. We sliced venison sausage from a local hunter, arranged crumbly cheeses on a platter, mixed simple drinks.

At the dinner table, we drank too much wine and passed the salad for the second time. My husband sat mute at the head, staring at his empty plate. His hands were folded in his lap, his legs crossed at the knee, fork and knife at a forty-five degree angle.

"Are you having fun?" I asked later when we pulled back the sheets. We slid in side by side, and I kicked my legs to get warm.

Sociologists have studied eyes at the dinner table, he told me. The people we look at even when they are not talking—when they are shaking the salt or wiping sauce from their lips—reveals who we love.

"So who do I look at?" I asked.

"You look at Jenny," he said. "You all look at Jenny."

"Because Jenny talks the most," I started to say defensively, but he was already switching off the lamp and rolling over.

Before he was my husband, before he sent me roses, Jenny and I were hanging around each other's dorm rooms, flipping through hulking CD catalogs and approving of each other's bookshelves. I noted the black-and-white photograph of Anne Sexton on her bulletin board and photographs of her friends back home in a park, wearing black sack dresses and huge sunglasses.

There was a snapshot on that same bulletin board of Jenny in a grand and voluminous taffeta plaid skirt, nipped at the waist. It had belonged to her great Aunt Pat, she said. I was always asking Jenny to tell more stories about Pat. We'd sit on the steps of our dorm, where we drank coffee and looked out at a wide, leafy boulevard lined with turn-of-the-century mansions, and she would. How Pat fled midwest heartbreak in the 1930s by sailing steerage to Europe—the apocryphal version that she was a stowaway. How she pursued painting instead of men, though men still pursued her. How Japanese diplomats sent her boxes carved from jade and ivory, how a famous novelist wooed her with a watercolor. How she was a great beauty, cruel and brilliant. We could never understand why art and all those lovers hadn't given her more pleasure, how she had died so angry and so bitter and so alone. Hadn't she chosen? What makes someone turn so sour, we wondered. We thought it had something to do with risk taking and with resilience.

Over the years, as Jenny's parents sorted through belongings in their garage and attic, I would sometimes receive care packages filled with silk scarves printed with scenes of Venezia, white horsehair clutches, black suede gloves edged in gold lamé, a robin's egg bathing costume, a green silk cumberbund-style belt with folds deep enough for stashing lipstick or a spare twenty-dollar bill. I loved the glamour of the items, and how they functioned in my wardrobe as both calling and warning. "We're unloading more of Pat's things," Jenny would write in the enclosed note. "And you're the only one who appreciates this stuff."

The afternoons were quiet. Laurie strummed a ukulele, Tommy was up in the high pasture again hammering nails on the one-room cabin, and Annie had exchanged guitar lessons for pottery classes from a neighbor. It was zero degrees in Soldiers Grove, but every day I left the house for a long jog. The runs were hard, the weather and terrain extreme. That landscape is an anachronism, a loophole in the surrounding topography, and as I ran, I imagined that I entered a portal to a frontier, one that would be more difficult to traverse but potentially more beautiful. I wore an ivory fisherman's sweater over my workout clothes and ascended a steep hill to a ridge with an old dairy farm. I slid on the ice, and at the base of a hill, a dog snarled madly until I passed from his view. I returned to Annie's feeling triumphant, my eyelashes frozen and legs numb. Upstairs, Jenny was reading in bed. I took off my wet sneakers and slid in beside her. Maybe it was the sudden change in temperature, or the exertion, but my feelings were right at the surface, like a leaf trapped under the thinnest morning frost.

"I had no idea life would be so disappointing," I said, and wiped my face on the pillow. She put her book down on the quilt.

"Seems to me you're only disappointed about one thing," she said.

"Then I guess I'm confused," I suggested. She turned on her side so we were facing each other and put a hand beneath her cheek.

"I don't think you're confused. I think you know how you feel."

The sociologists are right. I love Jenny's flat wide fingernails, the calm and assured way she navigates traffic, her untouchable *don't fuck with me* attitude at parties, and I love the Southern timbre of her voice, even when it gets slow and honeyed, which is what it does when she's about to deliver what's hardest to hear.

"How do I feel?" I asked.

"You're over it."

New Year's Eve morning. It's the best time of year for someone who likes imagining a better future, and my husband was sunny and warm. He poured me a cup of coffee and pulled me close.

"I know what my New Year's resolutions are," he said with a grin like he'd been up to no good. It had been so long since he had flirted with me, it felt sudden and inappropriate, like an uncle kissing me on the lips.

"Oh yeah?" I wanted to soften into his arms. There he was, finally. I was there, too. I leaned into him, felt supported by the muscles of his chest, the bones. He put his lips to my ear.

"I want to have a baby," he whispered, "and anal sex."

Before dinner, Tommy carried logs to the barrel-shaped wood-fired sauna so that its hot maw would welcome our naked bodies once we were full of black-eyed peas cooked with bacon and Annie's homegrown onions. Only the women ever made the pilgrimage up the snowy hill. We carried glass vials of chakra-clearing potions to dab on our damp skin and mason jars of cocktails. Inside, it was like a gypsy's caravan. Sweat beaded on our breasts like jeweled necklaces, and we told secrets in the dark. When we emerged, I plunged into the snow, and arced my arms and legs until there was an angel.

When my husband and I were on that happy Scandinavian vacation, we traveled to a nineteenth-century sauna built at the end of a wooden pier. He waited for me in the snack bar, and I pushed through the door marked DAMER. As I sat in a sauna with a square window that faced the Øresund strait, it began to snow. A swan glided past the picture window view, no joke. I liked being among the bodies on the teak benches. We were old and young, some folded with skin and age and others languorous, starlet-stretched.

I sat there as long as I could, skin scorched. The cold plunge was straight into the sound. I pretended to be brave and jumped. Just seconds of splash in the water, then hauling my body out on the ladder, my skin electric and burning, my mind slapped right into present tense.

E NOUGH TALK. To become the kind of woman you want to be, my mother said, you have to take the kind of actions that woman would take.

I LOVED MY HUSBAND, and then I didn't. Is that a story?

Story is giving a character a tangible desire, then putting things in her way. I wanted my husband to "be there" for me as my mother died. *What does that mean?* he asked for months. *To "be there"?* More tangible, he said.

Then my desire was for him to acknowledge my body, to hook an arm at my waist on the street, and in our bed, to press his torso against my back in the dark. Be there like that. We, at least, were still alive. Please, I said.

His desire was to not be told what to do. I began to cry beside him on the loveseat in our therapist's office.

"Is there something you could do now to comfort Sarah?" the

therapist asked. He looked at her like a student eager to have the right answer. He graduated summa cum laude, but I thought I'd had the better education. "I don't know," he said. I pulled another Kleenex from a box on the side table. "Hold her?" he asked.

"That's a great idea," she nodded, with gentle encouragement. He moved closer to me, draped his arm around my shoulders, and we looked at each other with proud embarrassment at this modest, remedial breakthrough. The awkwardness underscored— this was not practice, it was performance.

T WAS AN ACTION, but it was not the action of the woman I wanted to be.

He sat at the end of the bar in a Klos Nomi t-shirt and a leather jacket. It was late. That winter, I often stayed out late, telling my friends to go home, that I would just have one more alone.

What is it like to be a man, I asked, and when he answered, I replied that maybe I would like to be one. We ate free popcorn and white flecks settled in his beard. He paid such close attention when I talked, he forgot to close his mouth while he listened. A person will tell you everything within the first twenty minutes of meeting them, my mother had said. The trick is whether or not you're paying attention.

He said, Fish or cut bait.

He had kind eyes, and people have gone on less before.

You haven't made any promises, my mother would say to excuse any behavior in a relationship that was not a marriage. Only now I had promised. In our own selfish ways, neither husband nor wife had upheld their vows.

What if a man pays attention to me, and I like it, I had asked my mother.

And she had said: That would be the most natural thing in the world.

The wind tunneled down Third Avenue, icy from the waves of New York Harbor. He said, Let me walk you home. We made it three blocks up the hill toward my house before I stopped on the cold, dark sidewalk. I no longer wanted my own life, did not want to return to its quiet rooms and blank walls. We had never framed a single wedding photo.

His studio was filled with Walter Benjamin books and DVDs of dark Scandinavian police procedurals, a guitar, an easel, and paintings I didn't like. He spread a sleeping bag on the floor like a picnic blanket. With the lights off, he played the trumpet. Then we laid side by side like train rails. I felt blisteringly alive, and relieved I could still feel that way.

"It is so nice to look at someone else's face up close," I said.

I knew, at how true the words felt in my mouth, that it was my cruelest betrayal.

M Y MOTHER CALLED it the end of puppy love. My husband agreed but struck a word. It was the end of love, he said.

Once named, our terms defined, at least he could be honest. I kept my secret.

I consider it our last date, the night we sat in a dim neighborhood wine bar. It was the same place we'd celebrated Valentine's years before. I had given him a handwritten card, poorly but painstakingly designed. After he moved out, I found it among electronics manuals and a stack of junk mail. But that night long ago, he had arrived at our table with a bouquet of orange tulips. We drank in low candlelight that cast heavy shadows. An elixir of bourbon and admiration traveled the distance between us.

Now it was truth serum. "What would you look for in your next partner?" he asked, and the question took me by surprise, though my answer was as ready as his, both of them knee jerk and reactionary and mean.

"Sexual enthusiasm and someone really, really fun," I said. "What about you?"

He looked at me hard, level, dead-eyed.

"Loyal," he said. "Someone loyal."

WE BOTH SEEMED more buoyant on the walk home, unburdened from our postures of hope, from being on our best behavior. When I emerged from the bathroom, drying my face with a towel, he already had a black bag in his hand. For years, his signature fighting stance was a sudden, wordless departure.

I didn't mind the leaving so much as the silence. *Just say you need some time,* I'd ask, *or a walk. Don't just go.*

This time, he remembered my request.

"I want to leave," he said.

"I don't love you," he added. "I don't even like you."

SAT WITH my mother one winter afternoon in her kitchen. The snow was banked under the bay window by the table. It was easy to spot birds from our seats there, their colors vivid against a white canvas and the thin dark lines of tree branches. We saw a cardinal that day, and a blue jay. Blue jays are the bullies of the bird world, she said.

"You need to make a list of what you learned from your marriage," she said. "That way, when you meet the next guy and your mind goes blank, you'll know what to look out for." A magnet held an index card on the refrigerator. "Good judgment is based on experience," she'd written in black Sharpie. "Experience is based on bad judgment."

At the time, I wrote a list of vague qualities. Sense of humor, it said. Someone who is present and not postponing joy, it said. But what did I learn?

Events occur in time and space, singular alignments of a moment, a choice, a chance. To search for a lesson in the timeline is to pretend it is, in fact, a line—that life progresses in linear fashion, with its subjects gathering an accumulation of knowledge and wisdom applicable from one occurrence to the next. That is the effort to moralize our lives, as if they were folktales. I'm not convinced. She and I had always been more interested in meaning than plot, but a lesson is the merest articulation of significance.

"What happened," a man too young for me asked. And when I said, Same vision for the future, different ideas of how to get there, he looked disappointed. "I thought one of you might have stepped out," he said. He was asking for a story.

Condoms in jeans pockets are tangible but not the whole story. They signify all of the sex and none of the despair. The longer version, had I told it to him, would have gone like this: When I stepped in from stepping out, and shook the cold out of my coat and scarf and slumped into the bathtub, I still had bourbon on my breath and the memory of another man inside me. I sat beneath the shower and cried for the mess I had made, at the cowardice of the only rebellion I could muster. Sometimes I'd fall asleep on the enamel and wake when the hot water had turned cold.

Now my life was the cliché-ridden trash.

AFTER HE LEFT the hangers in his closet swinging, I pushed all the living room furniture to the center of the room and covered it with a rough taupe drop cloth. I wanted to paint.

In years of photographs from our dinner parties, the orange color on the walls had seemed warm, and with the low candlelight, our faces glowed as if we sat not around a dinner table but a campfire. But in summer, the color had always struck me as too hot—close and oppressive like a stranger's breath.

I chose a stark, matte hospital white. Night after night, I returned from work to the room that looked like a home long vacated, the furniture draped in white sheets. I painted by the light of a bare bulb, then sat on the ladder, exhausted, overwhelmed, scanning my eyes across the patchy walls. It was all taking so long.

Three girlfriends arrived unannounced on Sunday afternoon. "You hold her," Laureen said, handing me her one-year-old daughter. Katie looked at my last near-empty gallon. "You need more paint," she said. "Eggshell?" She left for the hardware store around the corner.

Jessica climbed the ladder and with her long arms carefully painted the seam where the ceiling met the wall. Laureen suggested painting the ugly closet door. I nodded, bobbing up and down with the baby. Katie returned, cracked open the can, and poured it into a pan on the floor. Before the hour was up, they pulled the drop cloth off the couch and pushed it nearer to the wall, then scanned the room, pleased.

"It looks good," Jessica said. "This is a cool single-girl apartment." The blank white walls reminded me of the Parisian apartments in Godard films, the emptiness a kind of shabby bohemian glamour. I could start to see it: I would lean my bicycle against the wall. I would keep oranges in a blue and white bowl on the table.

Jessica's husband arrived to pick her up, and jiggled my front door handle. "Do you have any tools?" he asked. Those had been my husband's, I said. He turned around and left, then returned with a screwdriver, crouched before the knob, and tightened screws.

I looked at my friends. Katie was checking her phone, Jessica had her hand on her husband's shoulder, and Laureen was suggesting how I might arrange art on the expanse of white wall now behind my couch. Her baby gurgled at my ear.

"Thank you guys," I said, and my voice buckled. "Thank you so much."

"Well, don't cry about it," Katie said, typing with her thumbs. I said that I would not.

THE LETTERS ARRIVED. They said, Congratulations. But maybe I should stay at my job, I thought, save more money, buy a cottage upstate. I was beginning to understand how people could hide from their lives inside the ceaseless demands of work. Yet it was becoming increasingly difficult to summon daily devotion for what had once been at its worst benign, and more often truly fun, and now seemed almost offensively inane. I consulted another food editor over fourteen-dollar cocktails. Maybe there's more to life than traffic goals, I said. Do we really care what the new quinoa is?

"Oh," she said, as if I'd revealed an adorable hobby. "You want to make the world a better place."

"Well, I'm from poor people," I said, since I thought that explained it.

"Not me," she replied, "I'm from money." I wondered how I should reply to this.

"I can't talk to other women like I can talk to you," she said. "We really should be friends."

On the walk home across the Gowanus Canal, telling my mother the story, I couldn't stop laughing. The dark water swirled with rainbows of shiny oil, the moon mirrored on its surface. I was as clear-eyed as a cat.

HAVE ALWAYS wanted a sense of self as immutable as a diamond, a fixed thing that refracts light regardless of outside attention or indifference. I'm not even sure this is how ego works, but I do know parents play a part in it, that a generous one can help give form to the inchoate shapes they see in their kids. Maybe this is why, in the months following my divorce, my mother kept repeating the story of my flying past her on the sidewalk the day I learned to ride a bike. She remembered I called over my shoulder, my long red hair streaming behind me. *Isn't it interesting? I taught myself!*

"You're turning into one of those New York women who knows how to do everything herself," my mother said that last winter. All I had done was driven us through snow to an Indian restaurant and suggest *saag paneer*. We listened to Joni Mitchell's *Blue* on the ride home. My mother nodded off, her head toward the foggy window, and woke to me singing. *I want to make you feel better, I want to make you feel free.* Her laugh was a mix of relief and pride, as much for herself as it was for me.

"See, you don't need me," she said. "You're going to be okay."

S OME OF HER FLAWS: She was helpless and avoidant. *Oh, I didn't get your message*, she'd say, when what she meant was she hadn't listened to it. She thought her tax bill a personal attack. She was both a know-it-all and an unreliable source, a dramatic arc more important than fact. *Oh, I don't know anything!* she'd demure if challenged. She whined. She was so practical she could be tone deaf. *But I love him*, I might say over a heartbreak, and she became a deli counter employee. *Next!* she said. And though she called my stepfather "pathologically optimistic," she must have also seen brighter things ahead. Days before she died, boxes of peony bulbs and rhubarb plants arrived in the mail. *I do not know if I have the energy to plant them*, she said. On Mother's Day, I dug holes for the peonies at the edge of the lawn, but they never bloomed.

S OMEONE THOUGHT there was an information blockage. That we weren't learning new details about my mother's condition there were to be learned. Someone called the oncologist, and all of us awoke to a group email the next morning.

"Anyone who calls the doctor will be permanently on my shit list," she wrote. "Do you think he will give you a secret prognosis that you can handle, and I cannot?"

Prognosis is an average. Prognosis, according to one opinion, said she should have been dead six months after diagnosis. I have never had the guts to call my mother's oncologist. I still don't want to be permanently on her shit list. There are questions I have about the end that will go unanswered. They have been supplanted by a belief as fixed as my DNA, inscribed perhaps with its own genetic doom. I think I know what he would say on the phone, his voice tender. It would not be about how she died but about how she lived.

I T WAS A crowded Friday night at a strip mall steakhouse after chemotherapy. A black hockey puck flashed to tell us our table was ready. My brother and I softened our edges with alcohol.

My mother ordered filet mignon and a baked potato. Growing up, she encouraged us to eat the skins. That's where the vitamins are, she had said. Now I noted she left hers on the plate.

"I'd like to be buried in a plain pine box like Johnny Olesen," she announced. "With a honeysuckle planted on top."

I sat opposite her in the booth, the beaded lampshade between us like the ones on horseshoe tables in an old movie big band supper club. Next to the salt shaker there was a laminated dessert menu with photographs of multilayered, whipped-cream-topped cakes and blue cocktails. This life is filled with so many distracting and crude details. I put down my silverware and looked at her across the table.

"I think honeysuckles are invasive," I said.

"Good," she answered, cutting a bite of steak.

spring
again

WE WERE ALL pulling away from one another by early spring, the veil between the living and the dead already falling. Why summon Bliss from China, my mother asked, when each of her children off living their lives was what made her happiest? We visited my sister for Easter. My mother slept in a hotel with my stepfather, where she stayed in bed, dozing, while Katy and I went to junk shops, took a yoga class. Saturday, we hid plastic eggs for my niece: in hotel room drawers, on windowsills, balanced on a roll of toilet paper. Violet searched, and my mother laughed.

My memory of the next day is vivid with color. My aunt had decorated the table with egg-shaped chocolates wrapped in pink and purple foil. My mother ate ham and green beans. Violet wore a yellow cardigan and a striped blue dress, both too long. Duncan practiced his Texas two-step with me across the pale maple kitchen floor. I drank espresso with whipped cream on top. It really was a beautiful day.

My mother and stepfather drove me to the train station after lunch. Everyone in the family was piggybacking on my Amazon Prime account, and it was up for renewal in August. Would she split the cost with me this year? Sure, she said noncommittally. I was flipping through a survivalist's homesteading guide someone had left in the backseat.

"Talk to me," she said, when what she meant was, *I have some things to say.*

This conversation I remember. It was when she told me marriage was Sunday morning and Tuesday night. That she was so proud I was going to graduate school. That I have only one life, and it is mine alone.

At the train station, I opened her passenger-side door, leaned in, and burrowed my face in her chest. I often felt afraid to touch her in the normal ways. I didn't know where it hurt and thought it might be everywhere. But that last time, I held her so tight. She wrapped her arms around me, I was subsumed. Her sweater was very soft.

As I waited on the platform for the train to arrive, I saw my stepfather watching from the station house. He stayed until the train came, and my mother sent me a text message.

"We want you to feel loved but not smothered. It is a delicate balance!"

A ND THEN THE veil fell completely. The phone at the farm rang with no answer, and she replied infrequently to text messages and to email.

"I am going to see *Alice Doesn't Live Here Anymore* with Jane," I texted on the way to the movies.

"That is exactly what you should be doing," she replied, meaning she was glad I hadn't come home for the weekend. When the movie let out, I wrote again. "Update: Kris Kristofferson is my dream man." She reminded me of the time we saw a handsome farmer in a hunter green MG, his dog's tongue flapping in the top-down Vermont wind.

"I'm worried about Mom," I told Duncan.

He sounded annoyed. He continued to bring her dinner, but he noticed with increasing frequency that our stepfather was the only one who ate. Has anything changed, he asked. But nothing really had.

What I didn't yet know but sensed, was the latest news her doctor had reported the previous week: she had months, maybe weeks, and certainly not years. This should not have even qualified as news to us, but it did. She told her book club in an email as they planned the next meeting, but she did not tell me.

"It is hard to express how much I love my life," she wrote them on Monday. "Please just make your plans, and I will endeavor to be there."

Don't be angry with her, one of her friends told me later. It is a mother's nature to protect her children.

On Tuesday she said I might consider taking medical leave from work to be with her. I was at home with a sprained ankle, learning how to use crutches. You just say when, I told her. Yet wasn't she saying it?

I did not recognize the event as it arrived; I did not take the action of the woman I wanted to be. I waited for a more urgent request. *Come to me now, baby*, I thought she would say.

But on Thursday morning, I woke to the voicemails Duncan had left throughout the night while I tossed and turned, unable to sleep.

"Sarah, Sarah," he said in one message after another, "please call me when you get this."

N THE NIGHT, my stepfather offered her a sip of water through a green straw, the kind wide enough for bubble tea. She began to cough, and what came up, based on the darkened pillow that lingered in their bedroom for days, did not appear to be blood but necrotic tissue. Her body was already dead inside. She coughed and coughed and she must have been very scared, and my stepfather, holding the cup with the green straw as her eyes widened must have been very scared, too. By the time the ambulance arrived, the event was long over. My stepfather says his two black Labradors, usually ill behaved and in the way, lay quiet and obedient as the men from the funeral home carried her down the stairs, holding her body in delicate balance down the winding staircase. My stepfather stood in the bedroom holding her gold rings in his palm.

E WAS FORGETFUL with grief. He didn't remember anything she wanted, and when the funeral home asked about embalmment, he said that was fine, go ahead. It changed her. It made her smell sharp, like a biology classroom. "Can I see her?" I asked. "She doesn't have any clothes on," the men at the funeral home warned. "She hasn't been made up. She's just under a sheet." As if that were not exactly what I wanted. This was the better time, when she felt more like she had been. But still it wasn't her. I knew that as I bent down to hold her. She wasn't there. Her body was hard and cold, and I nuzzled against her cheek and squinted my eyes to make the picture of her face a little fuzzier, because the face was wrong. It wasn't right. I don't know how else to say it. And I don't know if it was the fluid they filled her veins with or if it was just that all the animation was gone. And when I'd close my eyes at night, that's what I would see, that wrong face, that cold body. I tried so hard to remember the way she touched me, what it felt like when she was tucking the tag of my sweater inside the neckline or leaning down to kiss me good night. *I love you*, I'd say. *I love you more*, she'd answer, like it was a game I'd never win.

THE CLICHÉS ARE always embarrassing.

Like when I was sixteen and crazy about a boy who drove me to the seashore on our second date, then let my head nod onto his shoulder on the long drive home. I stood in the cafeteria the next day unable to sit at a table, my stomach too filled with fluttering to eat a sandwich. Butterflies. That boy is now a girl, I recently learned, and felt happy for her.

Grief is a mirror image of love.

At the funeral home, a man in a black suit told us where to send the obituary, and as he outlined the logistics, I wrote notes on a yellow legal pad taken from my stepfather's office. I was proud to be so competent in a crisis. When the man in the black suit began to list nondenomination cemeteries, my stepfather interrupted, as if there were important information he needed to contribute to this conversation. He began to tell stories: how he met my mother in the Williamstown Second Congregational Church basement, how they found each other again at a college reunion, and their second, second date in Paris—four days in a two-star hotel during which they rarely left the room. "If I had my choice," he finally said, "I'd keep her right here with my arm around her." The man listened patiently with soft eyes. "Thank you," I said about the cemeteries, "we'll check them out."

But as my stepfather and I left the building, I found I could not travel the distance to the sidewalk. My muscles went slack, and the scaffolding of my bones collapsed at the knee joint. On the front walk of the funeral home the afternoon my mother died, my stepfather held me until I could stand. I went weak in the knees, as they say.

IN THE CAR to scout our list of cemeteries, my stepfather said maybe we should put the funeral off for a month, maybe two. Dancing is Duncan's romantic side, but he is the most practical among us. He works in insurance and is able to say things no one else will. "There will never be a good time," he said. "Better to get it over with."

My husband wanted to pay the rush fees for our divorce.

"It is a cliché that the man wants a quick divorce," my mother had told me on the phone, "and then after it is said and done reconsiders."

But now I could understand: I did not want my mother's body hanging around for a month or two.

My husband and I split the cost, and I wrote him a check for four hundred dollars. He did not reconsider.

Lower Amwell Cemetery was windswept, with an empty, unlocked one-room shed with a broken window. This isn't right, my stepfather said. He lifted his chin to the grass on the far side of a low stone wall. A lawyer he wasn't crazy about owned the adjacent field. We opened the car doors, closed them again. My brother drove. The sky was ash gray.

When we turned into Sandy Ridge Cemetery, the car pointed straight toward a tall, upturned conifer. This wouldn't do either.

"Your mother hated red cedars," my stepfather said. The announcement was like a love letter to intimacy and to knowing, and it made me laugh. "Well, that won't do," I said. My brother rolled on between the headstones and out toward the exit.

One thing she didn't hate: Mexican barrel chairs. I knew that. Years before, when I was moving into my first Brooklyn apartment, we found a disintegrated pair at a garage sale on Kingwood-Stockton Road, directly across the street from Rosemont Cemetery. I bought a wrought iron fireplace screen to hang above my bed as a makeshift headboard and two glass decanters etched SCOTCH and GIN. She did not buy the chairs. They would have worked in Texas, she explained, but that was her old life. They no longer suited the style of her house now. It was my turn. I would waste sunny Saturdays with the man who would become my husband, gripping my fingers around the wrought iron scrolls.

"That's a marvelous redbud tree," my stepfather said at the third cemetery. It was in full bloom, the same electric fuchsia as the branches outside their bedroom windows. He sat on a bench dedicated to the memory of someone else. "I can sit here," he said, patting the empty wood slats beside him. He took two plots, side by side.

FAMILIAR COUNTRY SIGHTS: mice skittering across the pantry floor, snakes silent and sleepy in the garden, and silverfish leggy against the bathroom tile. Yet there was an unfamiliar country sound as I went to sleep that first night at the farm. The ruckus in my childhood bedroom was a trapped bird, beating wings and feathers. It was so out of place, so unexpected, like a clown waiting at the bus stop. I shut the door, though part of me knew this was cruel, and slept in my little brother's empty room. I was tired of thinking about others. I had never been so tired.

By morning, I choked awake with the memory of a body beneath a white quilt. Then my husband on the telephone. We hadn't spoken since the night he stuffed shirts and underwear in his laptop bag. It had been another season. "I thought she was getting better," he said, his voice blank with shock.

Time to deal with the bird. It would have been months since anyone had ventured beyond the sick rooms of the house: master bedroom for sleep, TV room for couch naps, kitchen for cups of tea. However long it had been trapped, this bird had managed to shit everywhere. On the blue and white Laura Ashley duvet cover, on the antique folding desk, on the changing table my mother had seen by the side of the road while driving home with my stepfather after lunch years before. *Stop!* she said, as soon as white spindle legs and a cardboard sign that read FREE came into view. She threw it in the backseat for a grandchild who had yet to be conceived.

While the bird flew from one corner of the room to the other, landing atop the tall bookshelves stacked with watercolor palettes and a hand-painted Japanese tea set, I threw open the window above the changing table. My two-year-old niece's unworn diapers were now splattered gray-green. And then—after all that furious flapping and wing beating, of crumpling collision into the ceiling and walls—this bird found its way out. It sailed through the open window with the purposeful ease of a button slipping through its hole. The room was suddenly still, and the panicked pace of my heart slowed in the quiet. It was time to mop.

"I still think Murphy Oil Soap is one of the finest smells in the world," my mother wrote at the end of an email that spring, apropos of nothing. Her houses had always been a wreck; Murphy Oil Soap was the fragrance of making things right. So I pushed and pulled the perfumed mop across the wide-planked wood floor with alternating fury and exhaustion. I dragged the bucket around the room, its water turning opaque as it filled with long, stray hairs from my sister's head and mine and dust puffs like season's-end dandelions. And then I found it. On the waxed floorboards beneath a west-facing window, another bird's body, stiff as a Christmas ornament.

This was country life. But that morning, it felt like something else—an uncanny death pileup, a haunting. The wooden mop handle slapped the floor. I went downstairs and returned with a white tea towel from a kitchen drawer. I wrapped the body and carried it down the long driveway, past my mother's order of peony bulbs and rhubarb plants collected on the porch, still in their brown packages. On the far side of the road, I opened the cotton bundle to drop the bird in its open grave and—who knows, maybe from blood or the stiff catch of its feathers or dried, brittle feet—the bird stuck to the towel. I stood on the side of the road, the one that led to the sloping graveyard where my mother would soon be buried, shaking the cotton fabric. The bird wouldn't fall free from its shroud or my hands, until finally, it did. It landed with the ceremony of another day's newspaper tossed onto the front step.

THEY ARRIVED WITH mops and buckets, yellow rubber gloves, vacuum cleaners, plastic caddies filled with cleaning products. My mother had been reading, and not reading, in a book club for more than a decade. Actually, she had been a member of two book clubs, each group discovering the other at the funeral like a secret family. That sunny morning, they walked toward me standing on the porch.

"Your mother would have wanted you to be comfortable in the house," one of her friends said. She had tried to send a cleaning lady over in the last months, but my mother had demurred, either embarrassed by the state of things or simply not wanting a stranger to rearrange what was, at least to her, the familiar order of her own chaos. "It was important to her the house be ready for you kids."

My mother had used that phrase a lot in the last year of her life, that she wanted to "get the house ready," that she wanted it to be "finished." She searched Craigslist for furniture and drove an hour to pick up free chairs upholstered in a dusty-red fabric she liked. When Bliss came home for six weeks between teaching jobs, she asked him to refinish the kitchen floors. He spent hot days on all fours, sanding small, hard-to-reach places by hand, and painted three different stains in side-by-side stripes for her to select the best shade. When she peeked into the kitchen to survey his progress, he wrapped his arms around her shoulders. They swayed back and forth while they talked, as if in the gym of a middle school dance.

The book club stayed for hours, the music of their caretaking filling the house: the rhythmic motions of the vacuum back and forth over the rugs, their feet up and down the stairs, the opening and closing of closet doors, the laundry room rumbling with what would soon be clean sheets on each bed. Murphy Oil Soap perfumed each room. When their work was finished, they gathered together in the living room and bowed their heads. *Allison*, they said.

THE FUNERAL HOME asked me to return with a bag of clothes for her to wear. The forever outfit. I chose the pink crocheted dress she wore to both my brother's and sister's weddings. "Crotch-et-ed," she had called it, imitating the saleswoman. Pompoms hung from the sleeves and the hem of the skirt, and she would shimmy whenever she wore it, shake her hips to show how the pink pompoms could bounce and bop. This span of time is liminal and uncanny: A person is dead but their body is present, and so we relate to it in the ways we always have. My stepfather said pack a pair of underwear for her to wear, too. "But she never wears underwear with hose," I said, and he said pack them anyway, it seemed like the right thing to do. When I told my sister what I'd done, she must have also thought of our mother's body as if it were alive, the comfort we still wanted to give it, how she would go into the ground wearing underwear she never would have worn in this life. "Poor girl," my sister said. I packed shoes, too: leopard flats with pink trim.

She left no instructions, just the snippets of things she'd mentioned in passing. I remembered the plain pine box and the honeysuckle bush. All the other choices were for us, not her. That I wanted her to wear a swipe of her favorite lipstick and to spray her with Ralph Lauren's Safari one more time, that Rick wanted her to wear underwear. And when I was upset about the embalming, which she didn't want, Jenny reminded me what my mother would have said in her high-pitched singsong. After that, every decision got easier. *Sarah, I don't care. I'm dead!*

One of those afternoons between death and funeral, when my sister had arrived and was changing her daughter's diaper by a bedroom window, a bee buzzed up to the panes of glass and hovered there. "Mom used to call Violet her little bumble bee," Katy told me. When I was in the bathroom that same day, I said, splashing water on my red swollen eyes and already wet cheeks, the lights wouldn't stop flickering. "Okay," I said, "*okay*," nodding at the light so hard, soapsuds still on my face. They are nonsense coincidences; they are messages from beyond. Both true.

My sister was very concerned about what the funeral direc-tors would do to her face. "Call them," she said, "you *have* to." I called from a PNC Bank parking lot. She didn't wear makeup except lipstick and mascara, I told them, so please don't use any-thing else. They told me about how her skin color would start to change. Maybe a little bit of blush then, I said. Sometimes you find yourself saying things you never imagined you'd have to say.

It took Bliss several days to fly home from China, which made the embalming seem sort of okay in the end. You put four kids in a car, and it feels like a party, even when you are going to see your mother one last time before she is dropped into the earth. Duncan drove. He is very left brained and logical, the savior of the unsayable again. He said, "Okay, who has seen a body in this state before?" I think he and I were the only ones who raised our hands. I loved him for asking that question.

The funeral home dressed her. I don't like to think about that. I brought her perfume and sprayed under the ugly blanket they covered her with and behind her ears, so that when each of us hugged her, it would feel more familiar. "Her perfume was a good idea," my sister said. "That was the realest part for me." My little brother stood over her body and read her a letter. Then he collapsed on her chest. I'd never seen him like that. Or my older brother, who, when he walked away from her body, doubled over and pressed his fingers to his eyes. My stepfather kissed her face again and again. My two brothers and my stepbrother and my sister and my stepfather and I stood in a tacky room while morose music played. I sprayed more of her perfume.

My sister turned to me. "I prefer the bumble bee," she said.

GATHERED BLOOMING BRANCHES of lilac and white dogwood from the fence at the edge of the farm and carried them to the cemetery. *It's good to wear red shoes on important days*, my mother had said. The heels I'd worn to college commencement sank into the soft May soil. I had worn a different pair on my wedding day.

The day was clearbright, cloudless and blue, and my family stood circling a deep pit on a hillside. A pine box was suspended over the hole, and I thought about her bones blunted against the wood. Against the dark earth, the pine was pale and pretty in the sunlight, like the white of an ocean wave.

When my niece began to cry, my sister gathered her into her lap and began to breast feed. I stood alone in the sun, only blossoms in my arms to hold. The minister read Edna St. Vincent Millay. My mother had carried a paperback of her poems to college. *How incredible, the coincidence*, I had thought. Now, I pity that girl on the hillside. She is so desperate for signs. Who doesn't read the sonnet that begins "I am not resigned to the shutting away of loving hearts in the hard ground"?

The talking finished, and there was not much, my family members took the lilac and dogwood branches from me one at a time and placed them on the lid of the casket. One blew off in the breeze. Someone picked it up and placed it gingerly again. The second time it fell off, they didn't bother. I laid my branches and grabbed a handful of dirt and placed it on top of the pale casket. That looked pretty to me, too, the black rubble of earth against the bare sanded surface.

THE PLAN WAS to sing Anne Murray, but Bliss warned me he would not be able to harmonize, despite our practice. My voice cracked at the first line. *People smile and tell me I'm the lucky one.* He joined in. My niece spilled her Cheerios on the creaky oak floor. *Even though we ain't got money, I'm so in love with you honey.* The full-throated voice of a woman surprised me. It was me and not me. It reverberated on the wood pews.

I cried in the white wooden church, and later, eating a ham sandwich.

"I am realizing," I told one of my mother's friends, whom I had never met, "that having a mother who loves you is a lucky stroke, like being born beautiful or rich."

"Arguably," she said, "a mother who loves you is the best advantage."

TO MYSELF I called it a "roiling" grief. I knew no other word to describe how I heaved: at the steering wheel, lying sleepless in bed at night, in the arms of anyone who paused long enough to offer a sympathetic look. The emotions were a testament and comfort. *Feeling is living to me,* to me, too. When the fit would end, I was hollowed out, scooped clean. Ready again to be full.

My therapist suggested group grief counseling, but I shook my head at the idea. Someone else might know loss, but no one could understand mine. My grief was special, singular, as all are,

unknowable by anyone who had not also belonged to my mother
by birth. Even among my siblings, we each had our separate ways.

Six months after her death, a relative by marriage approached
me at a party and began to cry. I knew him as the man who used
to sit with my mother in the kitchen after Thanksgiving dinner
when he'd had too much to drink. Once, as I cut a second slice of
pecan pie, I saw him lean close and whisper how much he loved
sex, how he loved to get sweaty.

She had made him feel so understood, he said.

"You think you're special?" I asked.

ANOTHER FRIEND WROTE another book and hosted an event in
a Brooklyn bookstore. The tables were crowded with her
hardbacks, cupcakes, and Champagne flutes. My friend wore
a stylish dress with an architectural detail at the neckline that
seemed to say *I am a serious literary author.* Her hair had been blown
out, and there were no empty seats. "It's so amazing to see all
these people from different times in my life in one place," she said
from the podium. She looked around the full room and leaned
into the slim microphone. "Hi, former boss. Hi, ex-boyfriend,"
she joked. Her face was bright. I felt so proud of her and so happy.
One day my name would be written on the chalkboard propped
outside on the sidewalk. *Tonight, 7 p.m.!* My dress would have
some kind of cool neckline, too. Then she stopped scanning the
room, and her eyes settled on a face. From the back, I could see a

sleek gray bob, the stiff collar of a starched shirt, a red silk scarf. It was her biggest smile yet. "Hi, mom." I was glad I could not see her face. I was glad my friend could not see mine. "You guys, she came all the way from Ohio."

FLIRTING FILLED ME up again. It pulled me from the edge of a deep pit on a cemetery hill and brought me back among the living.

"I think it's a blessing," my friend Jane said. "What are you going to do, sit home alone and feel the full weight of your sadness?"

Instead I felt the full weight of a man's body. David left oily sardine cans on the counter and fell asleep to a 12-hour YouTube recording called "Rain on a Tent." He sang "If I Were a Carpenter," and looked like he wanted me to harmonize, or answer. When he watered the neglected orchid on my windowsill, its green buds cracked into five-petaled blooms, their insides washed watercolor-violet, edges pale as a celery heart.

When I spilled bourbon in the grass and couldn't remember the words to the songs I love, he led me from one body of water to another. Down a wooded path to a creek bed swimming hole, to the ocean. We sat on a sun-bleached slab of driftwood, slipped out of our clothes, and tiptoed across the uneven stones pressing into the soft arches of our feet, down to the lapping edge, then into the cold water, rocks ragged underfoot. The day was bright, and we bobbed underwater like corks. I tilted myself back, held on the water's surface like a hammock. The bay was filled with moored sailboats, and then suddenly I couldn't stop laughing—at the sun on my face, the cold water stinging my eyes, salty in my mouth; at the man who stood naked nearby, as tall and stately as a heron. We waded back to the shore and I said, "Thank you thank you thank you, that was such a good idea," and he shooed it away. "Of course." The seat belts clicked, our hair wet in the windows-down wind. He said, "Let's go for ice cream," and we did.

Night after night at Long Pond, we watched the sun sink below the pines. The water reflective lavender, the sky soft pink, like a fingertip. I felt a duty to experience each pleasure twice—once for my own sake and again for someone who could not. My mother would have liked the cool of a Berkshire evening, the Irish fisherman's sweater I had pulled over my sundress. She would have found this cocktail too strong and too sweet. David stoked the wood fire in the evenings, carrying in logs from the wood pile out front, and she would have liked that, too—going in once the fireflies came out, the clanging pots in the kitchen as they hit the burners. After dinner, he sat in the stern of a canoe and paddled us from end to end, the oar dipping into the dark water. I sat in the bow, relieved to let someone else steer.

But if he left me alone for the post office, or to buy orange juice, he returned to find me on the couch.

"Why are you crying?" he'd ask, and I'd answer, "I don't know," because the truth seemed too long to explain.

I think again of that anthropologist on the radio, the one who talked about our brains under the influence of attraction.

Who wouldn't want to crowd out grief with something that feels like hope?

WHEN THE SUN shone, I tilted my face up to it and closed my eyes. God was not everywhere, but she was.

PLEASURE BECAME THE escape hatch to my grief. One friend was impressed by the range of men to whom I was attracted. A captain of the Staten Island Ferry, a motorcyclist, a cocky magazine editor, a bad artist, another cocky magazine editor, a barista, a sci-fi novelist with a trust fund, a Canadian, a surfer, a waiter, a bartender, a silver-haired architect, the writer I began to love. I had never done this before. *This*, being what I understood my friends had been up to in our twenties when I was playing wife and roasting chickens. Meet-cute in the dark, sniff out fun with a bourbon nose, feel your way. I loosened the valve in me that had been turned right-tight, and skin became my sail, directing me toward an island of relief. Witness: my forearm, my foot sole, my fingertips; the bowl of my hip bones, an earlobe, lower lip. Grief introduced an unknown abyss, just as it revealed the inverse, like the black-and-white trick silhouette of an old woman. Seen just so, she is young, too. And so a scrim parted, and behind that was a vast expanse. It could be saturated with the sense of something other than pain; it could be flooded with joy.

T HE LIGHT OF early evening, driving a fast highway at rush hour. I remember: "It is hard to express how much I love my life." I had heard this as a kind of grateful prayer. "I have not accomplished much in this life," she decided on her fiftieth birthday. "But I have loved and been loved, raised four great kids, and I still wear the same size I did ten years ago. It just doesn't *look* the same." Suddenly I'm in the fast lane, and I see her reclining in bed. She can't sleep, and so she is up weeping, pushing the sticky buttons of an old cell phone to send this last note to the women she has read novels with for years, a last note about how much she loves her life, and this time, the words ring in my ears with panic. The sound goes sour, like an atonal turn to minor key. What if it were not gratitude but a lament? I hear it then as a cry, the sound of a life pulled from its vessel. *It is hard to express how much I love my life. Please do not make me leave it yet.*

I WAS COMFORTED by my own grief. I liked to sob until my breath couldn't keep up, like staying underwater too long and then returning to the surface, panicked, disoriented, and then awash with relief. I liked working myself to exhaustion this way, heaving until I was scraped clean. I liked feeling that total and complete emptiness. It felt factual to me, like irrefutable evidence. This was how much we loved, now turned inside out.

WHEN I RETURNED to work two weeks later, I thanked my boss for understanding I needed the full time allotted by our company bereavement policy.

"We all understand," she said. "Sometimes life gets in the way."

She had it all backward.

Shortly after that, I gave notice.

I WAS TEN years late to being alone and began to note its difficulties one by one. I could not reach the overhead kitchen light, for example, and had never before bothered to purchase a stepladder; my husband could reach it standing on a chair.

My car was a culprit. Whenever I awoke to the gray slate roof of the church out my bedroom window buried under snow, I felt the aloneness. I felt it stepping into my boots and pulling on my gloves, holding the shovel, and then outside in the storm, stooped beside my tires as I tried to clear myself a path.

Imagine my relief to learn a friend hired a neighbor boy to dig out her car. And when I discovered I could climb onto the kitchen

counter and hold the top of the refrigerator with one hand and
reach for the overhead lightbulb with the other, I felt an outsized
sense of triumph. *How many divorcées does it take to change a lightbulb?*

Our marriage, in the end, had echoed with loneliness. How
many times had we been restaurant silent, the couple that dines
wordlessly, then beams up into the server's face at the offer of
more water and dessert? To feel the absence of affection between
us where once there had been so much, florid and overflowing—
that was lonely. This was just being alone. Empty rooms, carrying
the laundry, the bed so wide I began to sleep diagonally across it.
I could begin to wrap my arms around each instance, one by one;
I could get my sea legs on the ocean of aloneness. As a divorced
person it was not terrible.

As a daughter, it was.

HAD GIVEN UP on dinner. Not the activity of eating in the evening, but the meal as a recognized daily event. It was not a ritual
I was interested in partaking in at home or providing for myself,
and so I ceased to turn on the stove, didn't even make my own
coffee anymore. What I wanted was to be out in anonymous pub-
lic places or safe, familiar ones—on other people's couches, at a
bar with a strong drink and a sweet friend. My friends treated me
to expensive wood-fired pizzas and assembled complicated snack
plates piled with cured fatty salami, briny black olives, crumbling
slices of aged cheddar. They ladled homemade chicken soup. My
own kitchen had become a room to pass through after it was long

dark outside, and only then on the way to the bathroom, where the smooth curves of the bathtub held me like a crib.

The cross-streets in my neighborhood slope down to a view of New York Harbor. On the walk home from the subway, between the rooflines of Sixteenth Street, the water is busy with the white wakes of speeding ferries, the creaking, high masts of historical replicas; the Statue of Liberty stands at the center framed by cranes and low-slung barges. One evening in the spring, I arrived home before the sun had disappeared behind the milky folds of her massive robed figure. I tried to find a new way to name the sky's shade of old-fashioned sailor's delight. One thing I loved about my mother was her odd celestial observations. A certain moon was like a fingernail clipping, a sort of sunset like God winking. This sky was the saturated hot pink of a ripe fruit not found in nature.

When I stepped across my threshold that evening, I dropped my purse on the floor and found eggs in the fridge. Low heat, a knob of pale butter, and I stood for several minutes at the stove dragging the spatula in figure eights, tending to it, until I tipped the yellow eggs onto a white plate. That night, I sat on the floor of the hallway, my back against the wall, and I ate dinner. That night, I did not cry in the bathtub.

NOTE TO SELF, care of mom's Stop and Shop bag: "Sometimes I wonder that our six-year-old may be brittle," she worried about me. "But when I advise her to look into herself and feel her strength, she responds with jolly self-control and a temporary surge of self-reliance."

I sometimes wonder that I am brittle, too, that the ordinariness of the world that others seem to bear with such grace and forbearance is enough to break me. I feel joy today. I feel sad today. Ticktock, careening from frivolity to despair in the span of a week. Feeling may be living, but living like this is exhausting.

The evidence to the contrary is today. Or May 9, 2014. Or May 22, June 13, July 28, August 17. All of the days I awoke from the cool relief of sleep to the blunt force of my grief, or even a less acute awakening to the simple devastation of what had been lost. Predawn birdsong can break your heart. Still, I swung my bare legs out of bed, put the coffee on, moved through sorrow and joy as they came in waves. After a year had passed, my doctor praised me with a pronouncement that proved my mother wrong. We sat in a small office downtown, and he tapped at his computer keys under black-and-white photos of skyscrapers. "You are very resilient," he said. True: To bend to force and not shatter proves a kind of strength I did not know I possessed, and still, that surge, too, is temporary—all of this is.

THERE WERE DAYS when I thought my mother had given me a great gift by dying. Later, I was grateful for certain logistical conveniences, like one less household to negotiate at holidays or the freedom to move far away, but I do not mean that.

Here is a woman who fills her one small life. Not with milestones—birthdays, graduations, weddings she wasn't particularly good at. In fact, it wasn't until college, when people fussed over one another's birthdays with hand-drawn cards, a proffered doughnut, little treasures left like bird's nests outside dorm room doors, that I came to know the importance of celebrating those special days, too. For her, the anniversary was in the hour hand. Branches of bittersweet in the snow. The copper kettle on to boil. Beauty is the ticktock, and feeling it the pulse. There is no reward in the end, my mother said of parenting. The only reward, ever, is ongoing; it must be the day itself. *Would I like it?* she would ask of a movie, a restaurant. She is out for her own enjoyment and yours. Go ahead, wink with a stranger at the cash register. This is how to make the drone of a day come alive. You want something done, ask a busy person, they say. You want to know joy, ask a woman who swims against her own sadness. Opposites are most striking when held at once: bloom and rot, reverie and boredom, grief and joy. You are just like your mother, people say, and finally I know.

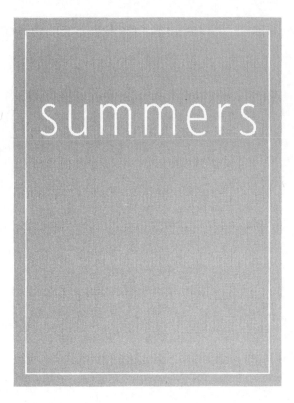

summers

J ANE DROVE ME to the farm the morning my mother died, and Jane drove me to the ocean in August when I was still crying. She let me be her mute and deadened passenger while she kept busy.

It reminded me of the picture book my sister had loved as a girl, *We Help Mommy*. We help Mommy prune the rose bushes. We help Mommy fold the laundry. On the North Fork, I helped Jane buy raw milk from a kind old Welsh farmer who handed us a glass jug and six brown eggs. I helped Jane buy a paper sack of square ice. I helped Jane shell beans and shuck corn, and eating outside next to the blooming hibiscus as big as a dinner plate, the salt air waving our hair, of course it was Jane who helped me. We walked into the lapping water of Long Island Sound, our hairless legs prickling at the salt, and when it was dark, laid our backs flat on the benches of the picnic table, still and silent, watching for something to happen, and knowing it was already right there, happening.

Jane gestured at the wide galaxy with her hand. That's Mars and the Big Dipper.

"This is how you feel now," she said. "Soon, you will feel something else."

I had only known one other person who could relax into life like that, could so take it moment by moment.

Inside, she flipped the downstairs lights off and the ones in the upstairs bathroom on. She combed her fingers through my hair, painted Jolene bleach onto a stripe near my ear and wrapped it in aluminum foil.

We piled into her bed, her laptop between us, and watched a movie about two women who run away together, turn tough and wild as she wolves. The lush 1930s wallpaper was like hiding in a tower of cabbage roses. She peeked inside my foil.

"It's ready," she said.

I leaned my head under the faucet and washed out the white bleach. In the mirror, Jane standing behind me, the white strands were like a feather woven into the underside of my hair or an earned stripe of paint across a warrior's face. *Look*, she said. Is this what a woman is? It is the more interesting question to me now. We called it my coven streak.

"We need berries," she said in the morning, and we drove toward the town at the tip of the island. First, a stop: a shaded street dead-ends at the beach, covered not with sand but with white rocks as smooth and round as eggs. We spread our towels and raked our fingers through them. Smaller stones the color of citrine and cooked shrimp, wet-shiny as marbles at the shoreline. We collected a little pile to bring back home to anchor the pages we each kept on our desks. The water was Aegean green with three jagged boulders that broke the surface near the shore. We dove from them like mermaids, waded, fought the undertow.

I was laughing again. Water and white sun my most reliable sources of joy.

"Our great mother," Jane said, and she was laughing, too.

Our limbs dried in the sun, and we packed up to buy berries and three kirby cucumbers. The beach stones were heavy in my bag. We drove with the windows down, hair whipping across our faces.

"When I met you, you were a girl," Jane said. Three years before, I was twenty-nine. It seemed another lifetime. "Isn't it great being a woman?" she asked. She turned onto the road marked NO TRESPASSING like she owned the place, and tree branches scratched at the car like bony witches' fingers.

I N THE FALL, I entered graduate school, driving an hour north from my apartment twice a week. I wrote in a library carrel with a view of the turning foliage and checked out stacks of books an armful at a time. I called workshop the dead mother parade, since I was not the only one who wrote obsessively about hers. There were dead husbands, too, fathers, pets, siblings.

"Are you in graduate school?" Duncan asked me, "or a two-year grief program?"

Both. I did frequently dissolve during meetings with professors, but my crying was as often about gratitude as it was about grief. When we sat around a table discussing Virginia Woolf as the first snow began to fall, I was acutely aware of what I was not doing. I was not buttoning my emotions beneath a starched collar or announcing myself on conference calls or analyzing click rates or writing advertorial about the versatility of a butter-like food product. I was no longer living my life in division. My heart, head, and body were in the same place at the same time, all pointed in the same direction.

I T WAS NEARLY Mother's Day again, and I stood in the cemetery under the afternoon sun. On the drive to New Jersey, I watched the vines of a yellow honeysuckle wave in my rearview mirror. It was the first time I'd been back, and it looked as it had that day—the sprawling purple redbud in bloom, the white dogwood at the base of the hill. It was a pretty spot, as far as death parks go. A man rode a mower up and down the hill. It was difficult to be maudlin in the drone.

When I arrived at the patch of lawn where I remembered we'd stood, there was no marker. I walked up and down the rows of dead, searching. There was no headstone with her name. We had not wanted to select one in haste before the funeral. The honeysuckle would do. Now it appeared this was an errand no one had wanted to resume or return to.

For most of the trip to the cemetery, my vision had been blurred from tears. The greatest comfort was imagining myself lying on the clipped grass above my mother's body. This spot seemed close—the angle of the sun and pitch of the slope. I split the difference between two spots that seemed like contenders, and tried to cover as much space as possible, sprawled like a snow angel. The mower buzzed in the distance, and a butterfly bobbed in the air. I wished I was the sort of person who believed that a butterfly was a sign, but since I couldn't, since I couldn't even be sure the bones beneath me were hers, since that quiet country graveyard was, at this very moment, loud with the sounds of upkeep, and of keeping on, I had to admit: It was all suddenly quite funny.

More likely *that* was her sign.

A FEW MONTHS later, between my first and second years of graduate school, I drove to visit my sister in Alabama where she had moved for a new job. "It was Mom's favorite magazine," Katy said, and it was true: I had found a copy on her bedside table, the recipes for coconut cake and black bean chili dog-eared. My niece had just turned three, and my sister drove us to the wooded grounds of her corporate office park to collect moss. We were going to make terrariums.

We had a spade, and Violet was very deft at separating the fluorescent green fur from the compacted, moist dirt by wriggling the trowel between the layers. She crouched thoughtfully in the same yellow cardigan she had worn at last year's funeral. It fit. My sister had cut Violet's blonde bangs straight across her forehead. "I got it!" she announced again, raising the trowel in the air with the moss in one large chunk like a green island. We gathered pinecones, and thin, spindly seedlings that looked like grown pine in miniature, like bonsai.

Violet is the first baby I have watched grow. It is like a little sister to say this, or perhaps like a mother, but she reminds me of me. It is her dramatic eyes, the way she widens them when she says, *You know what?* and the way she stirs up her listener before she delivers the payoff of her big news: that she can ride a scooter, or roll into a somersault, or has three best friends at school. It is also the way she can whir herself into a frenzy and is overcome, overwhelmed, by the intensity of her own emotions. Violet was spirited that day with the moss, and naughty, repeatedly careening near an edge of landscaping that dropped off onto a blacktop, far below. "Violet, stop," my sister said with a scary edge in her voice, and Violet screamed. She hated to get in trouble, to do anything wrong, and mostly she hated this voice from her mother. It was all familiar to me. *You are spirited*, my mother said, *and naughty*. Katy crouched and pushed Violet's bangs aside with a soft hand, her voice soothing again. "It is because I love you so much, Peanut," she said, "past the stars. I don't want you to get hurt."

Back at home, my sister gathered glass vessels from the lower kitchen cabinets. Inside each one we arranged a bed of moss, planted a thin, faint fern, and covered them. Sealed under glass, terrariums create their own gentle weather systems, pass time, and thrive in their own delicate atmospheres. It seemed an ideal model—that with the right conditions, they required little outside intervention to grow. We arranged the glass domes like emerald cities on the kitchen table. Violet and I rested our chins on our hands, folded on the marble table, and watched, amazed. Made small like that, anything seemed possible.

WHEN MY FATHER snapped the photos on the early evening
South Padre beach, he didn't know the brackish Gulf
of Mexico seawater had seeped inside the camera. It was my
mother's discovery at the counter at Eckerd Pharmacy, flipping
through a white envelope of blurred and out-of-focus photos, the
dusk-warm shapes as fuzzy as a skein of mohair. In them, she
stands on the low-tide sand with Bliss, then a toddler. She is long
legged and leaning over him, wearing a t-shirt from the elementary school carnival where she worked the pie toss in the morning, the dunking booth in the afternoon. She is shaking her finger
in a faux scold while he looks up at her with mischievous laughter.
Earlier in the day, sitting cross-legged with her in the sand eating cold grapes, I saw delicate, dark hairs like spider's legs escape
from inside her suit at the crease of her thigh. She loved the light
of those photos, and the serendipitous streaks. She handed the
envelope back to the developer and asked that they be blown up.
Framed, they joined the other photos in the hallway outside her
bedroom, including my little brother in a high chair, the bright
slant of early morning sun spotlighting his sleep hair, his mouth
full of ripe banana, eyes closed from laughing. Motherhood was
the highest art in our house.

THE JULY HEAT in Florence, Alabama, is an oppressive menace.
I am on my own cross-country adventure, nearly retracing

the route I saw from the cab of a moving truck as a kid. I am not *just* like my mother. This time, I am at the wheel and eat Cheetos and giant, expensive salads made of kale and sunflower sprouts, take scenic routes of my own design, pick up grocery sacks of used paperbacks in Southern cities. I stop at a junk store and purchase a white silk slip, a tire gauge, and a sugar bowl in her china pattern with money I've earned.

I stop at a Residence Inn for a swim, where the view is of Highway 2, a gas station with four rusted pumps, and a mobile park across the street. Some trailers have plywood leaning where windows should be. My swimsuit was once sexy, but no longer fits. I tug at the top and slide into the water.

I dog-paddle, dip my head back, and then two young brothers swim to me. The younger one wears inflatable wings. His accent is so thick, I can't make out a word.

"Hi," the older one translates. He is the age of not being afraid. His cheeks are red from a day in the sun. "What's your name?"

I tell him, and he gets to talking: he is five, his name is Davis. We swim around each other and splash for a while, and then I say, *Well, nice to meet you*, pull myself up the pool ladder, and drop into the hot tub with my novel. Then splash, wet pages, and Davis is suddenly beside me again.

"What's your book about?"

"Davis, leave her be." His mother, in short shorts and a t-shirt, is sitting at a table under an umbrella. I smile, tell her it's fine. She turns back to her phone.

"It's about Italy," I say. "Do you know where Italy is?" He shakes his head no.

"Italy is in Europe, on the other side of the world." He looks at me blankly, interested but unsatisfied. "It's where macaroni comes from," I add, proud of myself for this orienting detail. "And spaghetti."

"Shells and cheese?" he asks.

His brother slips in the water on my other side and touches my arm to get my attention. He is not yet afraid of anything, either. I am beginning to acclimate to his molasses singsong. I gather his name is Owen, that he is three years old but will turn four on July 27, which is in ten days.

Davis wants his turn again and reaches for my other arm. They touch me in an absentminded, easy way, not caring that I am a stranger. Davis arranges himself in my lap, and Owen strokes my wet hair. Suddenly they are my puppies, scaling my body with playful care, as if I am theirs. They want something from me, and whatever it is, I want to give it to them. Is this what a mother is? It is the closest I can come for now. Freckles stretch across the bridge of Davis's nose, constellations among them. I do not want a bad thing to ever happen to him.

"Yes, shells and cheese," I say, and Davis looks up at my face, ready for the next thing.

"Wanna get back in the pool?" he asks, and I do.

Acknowledgments

I would like to express my profound gratitude to a lifetime of teachers and to my Sarah Lawrence family, in particular. Jo Ann Beard, Jake Slichter, Vijay Seshadri, Brian Morton, and Paige Ackerson-Kiely showed me what was possible, and generously offered their support and friendship.

My family has been admirably graceful and encouraging of a writer-daughter-sister-niece to whom nothing is too private. I'm especially grateful to Katy Lukens and Madelyn Young for multiple careful readings and corrections of chronology and fact and for understanding, as Tobias Wolff wrote, that memory has its own story to tell.

I can never fully express my gratitude to Sarah Weir and Peter Grossman, who offered not only creative feedback and friendship but food, clothing, shelter, and a place in their family when I was most in need of a home. Thank you to Megan Bayles, Jenny Walton-Wetzel, Piper Weiss, Sonia Evers, Laureen Ellison, Jessica Cannon, Katie Melone, and Shane O'Neill for their friendship, endless brainstorming, and encouragement. I am also grateful to

Sarah Hepola, Siobhan Adcock, Amy Shearn, and Jessica Hendry Nelson for their meaningful pep talks at critical junctures.

I cannot overstate my gratitude to the MacDowell Colony, Ucross Foundation, Vermont Studio Center, and Virginia Center for the Creative Arts for their generous gifts of time and space. These places taught me about magic. Thank you, also, to the artists at each of their dinner tables who helped me grapple with the work as it was making its way onto the page.

My profound thanks to Gráinne Fox for her steadfast belief in my writing, unflappable calm, and wicked sense of humor, as well as Veronica Goldstein. At Liveright, I am grateful to Gina Iaquinta, Cordelia Calvert, Steven Pace, and especially Katie Adams. I wish for all writers to work with such a sensitive and incisive editor.

And to Max Hart, for margaritas, and truly, more than I can name.